Rob Vinciguerra

Table of Contents

INTRODUCTION

OF LOVE

Introduction of Love

This is "The Book of Love". A book of Love? What does that mean? What does it include? How can a book contain Love? All the answers are here. It is time to take a deep breath and prepare yourself for a journey to the depths of Love (as corny as it sounds you will discover a new meaning; a new truth; a new way of thought and logic to indulge into your brain with success that will impact your very heart to its limits.)

The word "Love" is such a strong word with such powerful meaning only understood by the heart projected by the brain enhancing the soul. To define "Love" is limitless but in reality, it is known to mankind as an emotion. An emotion can only be described through experience. Feel it, breathe it, live it, speak it, Love will set you free! Freedom of expression flows around this world but tends to flow on the inside rather than the outside at times. What you feel inside must be let out into the open so that you can clear the air of all the bottled-up pressure from bursting away. Control emotion and extract expression.

The power of Love will be shown in the pages of life. We live to discover what is in those pages and strive for the answers to questions that only experience can bring forth as time passes by.

This book will hold the soulful energy you need to target the truth within the pages of life. *Let the truth be told because Love will unfold as a sight to behold. A path is near to overcome fears, wipe away tears and find out what's clear.* Listen, relax and allow yourself to finally understand the true meaning of emotion, the ultimate emotion as designed by the one almighty, it is known to be "Love".

Now to stop beating around the bush, let's get into detail. Love started at the very beginning of time. How is that? How can that be proven? Well as many people can see, just look straight for one second........... There you go, this is known to mankind as "Life". Life was created by the one almighty himself known to most as "God", and some as "Buddha", "Allah", "HaShem", "The Source", and many names in various religions, but in this book let's refer to him as God.

Introducing Love to God is what's wanted from us. It is time to show Him that we have that power. To Love or not to Love, that is the question. A really stupid one. Love controls all that is good in this world. It will bring the good out of everyone and expose the real intentions of a person. From bad to good, we all have a reason. An example is "I killed him because he killed the Love of my life!" Good intention, very bad performance.

God always recommends non-violent acts but unfortunately instead humans Love to fight. It really should lean more towards "humans fight to Love" but not physically, mentally fighting through the struggle. All the obstacles laid out ahead of us are meant to be broken. Let's find a way!

Comprehending right from wrong is logically learned throughout the time which becomes later self-taught. As we grow up, we learn and understand moral values and what is precious to us. It is those beginning stages as a kid that impact our decision making towards the future. Our very own comprehension triggers Love to start playing a role in our lives.

As we grow older, we learn to Love, we understand Love and then we start to embrace Love. It is such a blessing alone to contain it in our lives and since we all do in some shape or form then we all should appreciate it as a gift. It really is our own job to introduce Love and our time to feel it, earn it, achieve it and believe it!

We as human beings are blessed to contain such emotion, especially the feeling of Love (being Loved, giving Love, falling in Love, experiencing True Love).

To live with such a blessing is incredible. We are lucky and don't even know it. More of us (even myself) need to appreciate life more. The air that we breathe, the sights that we see, the food that we taste and the sensation to feel. All these senses we have which we are allowed to use are all a blessing from God so that we can experience life at its fullest extent and become more successful for the future.

Future, let's talk future. The future is the key to the entire world because it represents us as human beings for the good or bad job we have done. We are living in God's playground so He can watch over us and guide us in the right direction so that we can overcome the hurt. *We all go through pain. We all go insane. We need to advance ahead and play the game.* He got tricks up his almighty sleeve. Let's see if we can all overcome what's thrown at us and move forward.. Don't forget we always are tested. Just like in school, if you pass the test you pass the class. You get a good grade and get rewarded. This was all a part of His logic and we subconsciously contain the basic elements we need passed down by Him so that We (humans) can pass His very own tests.

As a result of all this, it is Love that has the biggest role of it all. Passion is a form of Love and a very popular one too. We all are passionate whether we realize it or not. Even the people that do bad in this world still have passion, obviously passionate for wrongly doings such as being passionate to "kill" which is insane! Well it is up to the Good to influence the Evil to use the passion we are all blessed with. *Use it wisely, stay true, the sky will always be blue if life is surrounded by the Love of you!*

Accelerate Time

Time, such a powerful word? Why? Because we all have it. Time was invented to organize life here on Earth. It is amazing that the existence of our species evolved enough to create such an organization. To organize life means to organize the soul. What is meant by that? Well we as humans are a body fueled by our very own spirit, which is our true self. We are who we are and we are the energy that supplies the body to live in fusion with our heart and brain.

Time alone was invented to control the soul and allow it to freely show its full potential in life's flow. Without time the world will be one gigantic mess. I know it, you know it and we all know it. We as humans were created by God to make the most in life. We have such a high capacity level which allows us to fully achieve success. Time allows that, our spirit accepts that and we perform that. The spiritual energy we contain can be used for the Good and in an orderly fashioned manner.

There are times that the days fly fast. Minds power bodies to live long and last. We all live in the present created from the past. Understanding organized minds; living through hard times is designed to out shine a nonexistence mess to get rid of all the stress. Never can rest if a war is addressed, spitting on the rest; soliciting nonsense to take over common sense. We must realize what makes sense. It is Time with no expense. Survival of the fittest can appear real tense, but with organized lives we live at 100 percent.

Now to catch a breath real quick. Let's get into the necessities acquired in this world we live in.

Time is money, money is power, power is Love. Where did that come from you may ask yourselves. Well it's real simple, let's start from the basics.

Time is money because every minute counts. Not sure how things are around the entire world, but what I do know is that I'm from Brooklyn. Holla! I do know that life is a hustle and that everyone can be getting money in all shapes and forms. For the most part, let's try to keep our hustling legit rather than selling drugs or stolen merchandise. Every moment in life should be a little planned out because aside from us all "living in the moment" all the time, we have no choice but to evaluate decisions and create outcomes. Cause and Effect (which has a chapter of its own) is how this world runs. Let's run the game, make money, live successfully and respect Time for giving us the opportunity to begin with. From God's Will empowering humans long ago (maybe a little help from the angels, who knows) helped out life as an organized place to breathe.

Money is power because it controls the world (unfortunately). Time allows us to organize the world with money. Money runs the world because we all need to "purchase" survival (unfortunately). This is how life was designed by humans which God only allowed to see how things turn out in his playground. Since He controls everything, He is actually allowing us to take control while he watches over us to guide the way. Food, clothes and homes in these days exist with money, for the most part. To make sure we live a long healthy life, we need those three basic elements needed for survival in these times. Survival back in the day before money, forget it! Hunting, fire and caves seem to pretty much fit the description of animal life in the wild which humans started out with. The evolution of the mind allowed us to get out of those elements, switch it up and live great luxurious lifestyles not even imagined in dreams! What may have appeared of such amazement back then only appears normal now. Money now exists and technologically runs the streets! (As said by a dude from Brooklyn.)

Power is Love? Seems like a new one compared to the other two. Well yes power is Love all the way since Love brings us all together and impacts the occurrence of success. Love technically controls everything, including Money and Time itself! Now that is deep. Let's talk Love! Having such a strong passion or strong emotion towards anything makes us want it more or want to do it more. Our inner strength is empowered by the Love we emulate. The heart is the holder of Love, the brain perceives it and our soul releases it; showing the power behind it all.

Remember this, "We have the power!". It's all about how we use it. Just like Bruce Banner, we contain the Hulk. The Hulk is incredible and it is within us. Whenever negativity enters our path, have the mindset of Hulk. "Hulk Smash!" right through the negative demons in our way and break through the barriers of time so that we can lead the way.

Allow each fragment of Time to become a memory and be a part of something you Love. There are good memories and bad ones. Use them both as energy to influence the present to achieve a desired future (which has already been foreseen by God almighty himself). We as human beings must obtain the ability to continue what has already been started. The creation of Time involves pressure to beat the clock when especially procrastination comes in play. "Know your role and shut your mouth" as The Rock says. We must understand what's really going on here and "Just do it" like Nike. "Game over" as said by Jigsaw from Saw. No more horsing around, let's get serious. "Can't stop till you get enough" as said by the legend himself, Michael Jackson. *There's never enough with handling all this deep stuff. Must keep it real; must act real tough. We don't have all the time in the world; it's real and rough. I'm pretty sure all these quotes enthusiastically caught your attention enough.* Now let's get deeper into how Time can be accelerated.

Imagine living in a world where such technology exists involving Time traveling with a government program created in the movie "Déjà Vu" with Denzel and "Looper" with Bruce Willis. Also, imagine having the power of Time in "The Time Traveler's Wife" with Eric Bana and TV show "Heroes" with Masi Oka portraying space-time manipulator Hiro Nakamura. Time in general is so powerful that it can defy everything, especially Love.

It is mind boggling to live with the what ifs about the possibility of being in Love with someone else or a possible other self-living in a parallel world where you are in Love with someone else. That is way too much to intake. It is best to live the life you choose and make the decisions you desire because there is no going back. Living with regrets can be a lot to handle so better off living with none. Let Love into our lives by embracing Time and controlling the present.

Accelerate Time; it runs through a clock. The days go by and never will stop. The seasons go by; cold and hot. As the years go by, appreciate what you got!

Growing Pains

Start off young and grow up to be old. A whole life story the way it should be told. Now listen up here, we have a priceless soul never to be sold even if Love is on hold. Temptation may lie around the corner; side to side, Love resides in the depth of our eyes where sight is disguised with motion through the lies. The truth lies outside and Love grows painfully deep inside.

From when we were kids, we wonder how our future life will be. Having fun with Super Nintendo, Sega Genesis, Marvel and WWF (WWE) action figures, drawing, playing kickball and manhunt as well as hanging out with friends are a bunch of activities I have done as a kid growing up in the 90s in Brooklyn. We all have our own fun especially at our younger stages in life, literally the longest period of fun as can be until we are older and retired. At that point we have fun just watching our grandchildren have fun. What we all know in life is that we all "Love" to have fun.

Puppy Love is what we all experience at these young stages in life all the way up to High School. We still experience pain when we are dumped by the person we "Like". You already know back in the school days it came down to a "Do you like me? Yes/No. The Puppy Love phase is there and for all of us to experience. It is a must, only to prepare us for the next stages of Love that lies ahead of us. To "Like" someone is mainly based on attraction which leads into feeling based emotions as a person gets older. The preparation of those elements will someday lead into a better understanding of Love, especially True Love. This will all come as the mind develops into a more emotionally intelligent asset towards that path. The mind must be more equipped with the tools to handle such future emotional pain that is included in the process of Love.

As we grow, our minds grow. We all know we must let it shine though. Spreading knowledge will continue to flow. We show how much we know through experience we earn. To grow is to learn and to know is to burn; burning the youth away. We stay fresh as clear day and advance in life another day. Enhance our heart someday and then say "I just fell in Love today!".

It's real deep stuff to say "I Love you", especially when you mean it. Starting off in the "Puppy Love" phase to only end up in the "Love" phase is the real deal and it all falls into the "The Stages of Love" which has its own chapter.

The pain is insured when you first Like someone and get turned down. It's like you got your new gadget/toy and it broke or was taken away from you the second you got it. The same concept falls into the category of getting turned down which happens to all of us no matter how confident we are or how tight we spit our game. In the end there will always be that one person that will turn you down and as some will just move on to the next, we all get affected by it in some way. Even if it was something little, we were affected.

Affection and connection with mind blowing exception. Yes? No? Maybe? Answer the question. Feenin' for attention; heart pounding depression that ends in one incredible selection. The choice has been made and Love was just mentioned.

The answers are already there. As we grow older, we enhance, advance and hold our stance. Intelligence will drive us towards comprehension of the Loving sensation. All questions will be answered in a matter of logic and moral values that confirm the validation of reason and purpose. Reflect on the past, handle the present and prepare for the future.

The older a person gets, eventually they will want their youth back. Memories and flashbacks kick in at all times, random times. *As you grow, sometimes you will reminisce and embrace all that you miss.* It's ok to never forget but understand that you must continue on with your life and move forward. Remember that we live in the present, not the future or past. We live to create a future, not create a present or past. We use the past as a tool, not the present or future. The tool is used to create a future that we live for. We are living in the "now". Let's not live in the "then". Now is the time to grow!

Enjoy every moment of your life from when you are a kid playing games to an adult drinking beer. Unfortunately, these times do not last forever. We can make memories last forever if we choose to and our goal should be to live this life the longest as can be. Live it to the fullest and prepare for a possible afterlife if it does exist. *The unknown will be known in the future passed our time that we eventually conquer on our own.*

You are not insane if you believe things that others don't or follow a religion others don't. To be honest, in humanity we as humans actually do need to be a little open minded so that we can at least understand the other mind to become more team oriented. If everyone joined together, we can change the world. Unfortunately, there is that one person that wants to be better than everyone else or disagrees in some decisions which may have a huge impact. Recommending and voicing opinions is perfectly ok but when it turns into a heated argument, that's when all the problems start. In life, we will deal with this automatically as of today's society which results in the natural Growing Pains.

Our time has risen with a visionary mission to create an incision that will prevent heartless decisions. A new way to make it ok to overcome sins; defeating the demons that devour us from within. Never the same to play the game, a one that should have been. A new gateway leading something new to begin.

     Never forget who you are and always become a star. A Love is out there waiting for you a distance from a far. A Love that is so true, a Love that completes what makes you you. Patience is the key, be yourself and nobody else. *The truth is real and growing through the pain will make you stronger and make you sane.* Continue on through life.

     Growing Pains, gone insane, control, maintain, continue, retain and a Love that you must explain. Don't complain. Let it rain. Let it shower. Minds expand passed the hour. Growing up real sour with piecing pedals to form a flower that spreads and towers the dirt. Enhance what's hurt and romance the Love that we have on this Earth.

Cause and Effect

For every memory there is a moment. For every step there is a path. For every decision there is a consequence. For every Cause there is an Effect.

Understand your surroundings, understand reason and understand purpose. Everything going on around you is happening fast. You must keep up with daily reasoning in the best of your ability to maintain a steady understanding of life. We are always tested with situations and events that may appear really good or even as an obstacle. Whatever the case may be, there must be a reason for it. We are all created for a purpose and the things we do happen for a reason. The littlest things we do can have the biggest impact on something else. *Make sure everything is well analyzed and instinctively correct based on what is to be the destined Effect.* The good, the bad and the ugly. Let's lean more towards the finger licking good.

We are all infected, connected, suddenly injected with Love growing strong to be known and well respected. Listen, think and pause. What is the Cause? It is time we must affect; thoroughly select the right choice of intellect to complete the final Effect.

Love will always be the ultimate Effect. It is the power of the

Cause that will create what's next. We must always not expect everything that lies in front of our very eyes because nothing in this world is factually disguised or predicted otherwise until proven true to the world and you.

What is Cause? What is Effect? What really should be the question is Why? Respect the decision and understand the result. There was a definitive reason for the happenings. Think about it. Stepping on an ant could change the world and little do we know it we already have. A clear example is in "The Simpsons' Treehouse of Horror V: Time and Punishment". Homer transports himself to prehistoric times where he realizes he must be careful because if he affects anything in the past, it could change the future. After swatting a mosquito, he returns to the present to find an imaginary community where Ned Flanders is now the dictator of the world. This is a world where accidents happen and mistakes are acceptable as long as we learn from them. Let's not make mistakes that destroy lives but mistakes that better lives. As known on anime "Dragon Ball Z", Vegeta states that a Saiyan gets stronger after every battle. We are in a battle with life to reach the strength we need for a successful future. What doesn't kill us only makes us stronger. *We need all the strength we can possibly get to take Life head on and make it our best.*

There is a known theory called "The Butterfly Effect". This theory concludes that by one occurrence, another occurrence happens elsewhere as a result of one Cause. Cartoon Network's Adult Swim displayed a funny sketch in stop-motion animation show "Robot Chicken" where a young boy tries to explain the butterfly effect to a young girl. When the young girl squishes the butterfly, it causes earthquakes in Japan. A Japanese woman retaliates by stepping on a butterfly, which causes a volcano to erupt behind the children. The boy retaliates as well by ripping a butterfly in half, which causes Godzilla to terrorize Japan. It shows stupid humor which exaggerates this theory. In many cases, minor actions in the past can have major effects on the present time. In the movie "The

Butterfly Effect" with Ashton Kutcher, it exemplifies that but in the life of the person creating those changes rather than life on a global scale. Every time he attempts to re-do his past to be with the woman he Loves, it changes his whole future. Those are two different examples of the logic behind that theory. This brings us simply to the fact that if you think critically and act fast then we can actually control our own future, possibly the future in general. Unfortunately, we can't control destiny, but a good portion of our future will happen because of us. Let's make it happen, let's all become successful and find the Love we dreamed for!

There is a Cause that could be so dark. Can't pin point the darkness shadowing the sea like an arc. An Effect so evil that will drop jaws like a shark. We must create a good Cause like a walk in a park with an Effect of great height that the world will see the light through the heavenly vision that gave us sight.

To be the Cause of something is very important and life changing because the Effect can be either good or bad. The impact from the Effect can actually affect the world. Make sure that you are well aware of what's going on so that the result ends up being a good one and not unaware of a bad one. As long as someone tries to make things right then there is a better chance of it coming out right. What's right is good and what's wrong is bad. No one should sadistically assume right for being bad because then that is when bad things in this world happen. Let's focus on the Love and not the hate.

Love can also be seen as a Cause. *What's done is done, in some cases, Love was the reason second to none.* What rules apply to it? Death can be an Effect from Love. Death has a chapter of its own. *So much to discuss, the importance is a must.* One tough situation that applies to everyone's thinking is "He/She killed the man/woman that I Love! He/She will die!" Now logically, some of us literally would want to kill that person ourselves even as kind and sweet as we are. Others will not even consider death as an option due to how kind and sweet we are. *It's all based on logic, it's all based on morality even though a change in heart can flash in the blink of an eye as an unexpected reality.* No one can expect the outcome of what comes next. So therefore, we must definitely make decision making a really important asset to our lives since those results are responsible for those accountable. Even though Death exists just for the simple notion of the world getting over populated; in the end our decisions are the ones that really have a message to send. Let's make them good ones.

Cause and Effect; a past to reflect. There are obstacles to deflect and a time to connect. Live with no regrets only to accept our life as it's kept. We live another day and take advantage of what's left.

BUTTERFLIES

Chapter 5

Butterflies

"What is Love? Baby don't hurt me, don't hurt me, no more" as said by Haddaway is a classic. A song loved by many but really makes you think, what actually is Love? Love is an emotion not a definition. What is felt can't be defined but only expressed. Expression to the fullest potential of emotions gathered together releases an aura of deep sensations from within.

"Girl, you give me Butterflies, inside, inside, inside" as said by MJ. That is the only true song of its kind that talks about Butterflies well known to the public, well at least for me as the most popular song on that topic. Butterflies, what actually are they? They are however you want to perceive them as. Well I felt it and I can actually describe my version of Butterflies.

Golden butterflies glistening with light and sparking through your stomach is how I see it. They fly around and bunch up together forming a glowing ball of golden butterflies once you feel the true sensational emotion known as Butterflies. Then they burst in all directions releasing that intense deep feeling felt once they were all bunched up. Now that my friends are how I feel Butterflies. Everyone has their own imagery and emotional concept, this was mine.

The intensity inside awakens your heart from a long sleep. It may have felt like dreaming and counting sheep, but the dream was over. Such a feeling; so deep. A Love has been created for us to hold and keep.

The feeling you get in your stomach from the Butterfly sensation represents how you feel about a person. *That is passed attraction but a true heart interaction. Stand up and embrace the smile on your face. The tears dripping inside an emotional space aiming in the direction of Love brought outside to inspire the whole human race.*

Sometimes it is hard to describe how you really feel, but when you feel how you feel you will know how you really feel. It's ok to feel some type of way. Just understand it and accept the emotion involved towards appreciating the present. *Some people find it hard to admit how they really feel but once your expression is let out, the relief is what it's all about.* Keeping it real pays off because at the end of the day you really want people to like you for who you really are and not who they think you are. *Seeing is believing, expressing is achieving.*

Everything in this world is unexpected and nothing can be predicted as a premonition because it will never turn out exactly as the vision. As life starts to unfold, we have our own story to be told. We must become the successor and provide guidance to others towards the right direction. Let's work as a team and help everyone through that fork in the road. Meet me at the crossroads as said by Bone Thugs & Harmony. Once we reach them, we must never forget them and utilize the knowledge obtained from these experiences in that path to direct us to the right one, the path of success.

There is a thought process when it comes down to having feelings for a person, you can't get them out of your head. It is said that haters can't get the people they supposedly envy out of their head. "Hate it or Love it" as said by 50 Cent. That image is still in your head no matter which way is felt. A different emotion and feeling in your stomach are the result of whichever direction of sensation or rage that takes course. When I have an adrenaline rush, I get this feeling in my stomach that makes me feel incredible like Hulk and have knockout power like Tyson. The human stomach in particular to me seems like a chamber of emotion.

Don't hesitate to learn. An emotional learning experience will take turn to resolve concern, break the ice and burn. Everything that happens takes its course to create a lead for a follower ambitious enough to become a leader. In order to become a leader, you must become a follower to learn and grow strong for the knowledge of power.

Everything in this world is based off of pure emotion, set and done. Dancing around, having fun and playing outside in the sun. Taking that trip to the park for a simple run or that sudden burst of energy that just made you feel so empowered, second to none. The best feeling may overcome the worst feeling just in time. That could have disrupted your mind and could have crossed the line but had a likelihood of just killing time. Nothing can be better than a closed mind opened to the possibility of such feelings in your stomach encouraging you to create adrenaline intercepting your very own life line. Utilize the Butterfly sensation towards appreciating how good it feels to experience Love every time.

This all brings us down to the feeling we felt in our stomach, Butterflies. The generalization of a fluttery feeling in the stomach is a reaction of stress when nerves kick in. This is a result of the release of adrenaline. It causes rapid heart rate, increased blood pressure and improved circulation in your muscles. One way that it can simply be felt in the beginning is a basic attraction, but once you reached the true experience then it is definitely now an emotional based feeling. An example of this sensation in your stomach may occur if you have the "Final Exam" coming up and your worried because you barely had time to study. Another example which is what this chapter is really about deals with a male or female you like that is nearby and you want to say something, but you don't know what to say. *Walking down the road, walking down the street, a feeling so good that you'll be swept off your feet. A feeling so grand to feel large at hand. It's time to embrace it and take a stand.* Even though your heart is in your chest and your brain is in your head, it must be soulful energy fusing the heart's emotion with the brain's feeling creating those golden Butterflies (as imagined by me).

Butterflies, fly and glide. Slip and slide all inside. Emotionally hypnotize the mind to find a Love outside. Cannot hide; a feeling felt deep inside forming a ball of light so bright. Butterflies shine day and night. Seen by the gift of sight. Held in the stomach so tight. Bursting out with no fight. A Love so real. A Love that is felt with such emotion to make a heart melt.

Concept of Theory

How can one theoretically prove? Prove what? *An opinion? A fact? A concept to be exact?* How about we conceptually discuss theory. Theory appears as a synonym for Opinion. Opinions are known to the world as unproven facts. Yet how can one prove a fact? Real easy answer, well it really isn't. I have said this before in the past. The sky is blue. It really is, it can be proven, all you do is look up and Bam! A blue sky in front of you. *It's not always blue, but blue describes it for what it usually is and as popularized as publicized and scientifically televised.* Blue is the dominant color for the sky. Well is it? I can prove right now that it isn't and by me proving that, what really is a fact? The sky is blue as said by People. What about animals? Well that is a mystery itself because even if scientifically studied or analyzed, no one can really know unless you are seeing through the eyes of an animal. But what I do know is that there are some people in this world that are color blind. That's right, color blind. To be color blind obviously means to lack sight of color. Even though the average person sees the sky as Blue, a color-blind individual sees the sky as Gray. Gray is even more dominant than blue in that case and overshadows the popular Blue color as seen by the majority of the human race.

Everyone is entitled to their own opinion. When it comes down to couples, friends will always give mixed views based on how they feel about the situation or sometimes the person. "She is not the right one for you" can be said by a friend that is jealous of the fact that their friend found someone decent and they didn't. But yet another person can say the same thing but only because they personally don't see them good for that person. Where I'm trying to go with this is that everyone is opinionated and Is entitled to their own opinion. Since opinions fall into the category of theory, that pretty much means that everyone can have their own theory on Love. The concept of Love will always be the same but the theory can be different. Discussing True Love will be as close as legit as can be even though others may think differently.

Love to discuss; lust appears as a must. New and fresh not to rust with a time to adjust. The center of the crust is where Love resides within desired eyes to create something more of greater size. Such a reward like a huge prize is deserved by the ones who earn God's Will to rise.

The conceptual thoughts of knowing versus unknowing all leads up to what's real and not real. It may appear that Love is a fantasy world and your living in a fragment of your own dreams. They say fairy tales come true. They do but for some, not for all. As shown on MTV's Catfish, there was this girl talking to some dude on the internet for a year and had strong feelings for him. Long story short, when she went to finally meet up with the man of her dreams supposedly, it ended up being a jealous girlfriend of her ex. Her dreams were shattered, she was living in a fantasy world.

Dreams aren't real but some people would like them to be. Sometimes things don't go the way that they hoped for in reality but when a dream is better than reality then who wouldn't want to live in that dream. Dreams are images, ideas, emotions, and sensations that occur in sequence unwillingly in the mind during certain stages of sleep. The content and purpose of dreams may not definitively be understood, but inspiration and reason may occur as a result. When being sucked in a different realm clearly out of the norm, that is which differentiates a dream from reality. Certain things in dreams just aren't scientifically possible to happen in our time let alone at all. When a person says they want to find the woman/man of their dreams, it doesn't literally mean they had a dream about them. It is the whole logic of a dream not being real and the woman/man that they hoped for actually being real, standing in front of them. Dreams represent unreal creations in the mind which make it a whole new world. I remember watching a documentary on TV which literally showed people on these beds hooked up to some relaxing machine which allows them to dream for long periods of time, giving them the opportunity to live that second life. We as humans are brought here on this Earth to live our physical life, not in the world of "The Matrix". So, let's live it the right way and allow the good dreams to inspire us and the bad ones to better us. The woman/man of our dreams will come true, we must allow Time to not overwhelm us and live life the best we can up until that day comes which will make our life even more meaningful than before.

Dreams, themes in a mind of schemes. The concept of what's real isn't really what it seems. Many theories put on screen isn't the same as projected beams from the mind scary enough to create a thriller and scream. A nightmare transformed from a frightened scare into lingerie wear to feel Love in the air.

It's never good to assume what is to be presumed as a moment passing soon. Too many people rely on prediction rather than actually thinking out the process. Never judge a book by its cover but by the pages in it. Read people rather than judge people. Depict a person as a book if that will do you good. Everyone has their own personality and unique sense of style. Belief and theory reside in everyone's mind and is a choice to become close to those of different thoughts. Having things in common and not in common all creates chemistry. It is conversation and attraction that will create the first stage of Love.

It has been theoretically proven that Love exists. Find it or let it find you. Regardless, it is out there and waiting to happen. *Happen now or happen later, Love will make its way and become the ultimate flavor. There is nothing like it out there, so enjoy it while it lasts or hold on to it real tight and never let go. Go with the flow, time to show a process fast or slow. Allow emotion to glow and a Love to grow.*

There is Theory. There is Concept. A place to be where minds intercept and hearts do connect on a worldwide context. Breathing life into what's next and prepare for the next step to show the world your rep. A test from God you must prep. A soul to lead after death. Forever Love to be kept. A new life to live in such depth. The heavens speak on our progress of our Love process that we must process to internalize whether it's now or never to let Love proceed onto the next level. Make emotions pour down as you pull the lever. Inspire the world with a Love created that will last forever.

EMOTIONAL ORIENTATION

Emotional Orientation

To Love your boyfriend/girlfriend versus mother/father is a different kind of Love. The strength gathered by that Love from family will benefit the Love for your significant other. The comfort and Love from family oriented gatherings enhance the happiness of the significant Love for your man/woman. They say "Happy wife, happy life". It is real when happiness comes in play. Happiness is the key, once you are happy you are good to go. Nothing can get in your way when positive energy is flowing through your veins. Let happiness in and consume it's joyful goodness until your very heart is steaming with Love.

Emotions definitely come in play when you Love someone. When a person feels deep feelings or pain towards a Loved one, most will tend to get emotional. Death plays a big role in emotion. If someone you Love dies, pain will be felt and even if there is great strength within that person, tears can still come forward. The adrenaline you feel if you witness or find out someone hit a Loved one is super strong and can cause severe damage if not controlled or handled properly. It is intense when you feel something deep inside. *You can't control how you feel, you can't control what's real.* You have reached an orientation through the first stages of emotion.

Emotion, devotion, so much commotion. Emotional breakage releasing deep water forming a spiritual ocean. Spreading inside your body soft like lotion. So smoothly in motion with natural indulging of a secret Love potion causing your brain to widely open and understand the meaning of Love as it's unfolding. Accept your feelings, embrace what it's holding. Visualize what's truthfully noticing in your own world of boiled up feelings and emotions.

Such deep feelings are felt just by having that emotional connection with someone. It really gets to you and makes you not want to leave but remain communicating as long as you possibly can until your day is done. *Building chemistry with conversations to sensations cause a surge of Love to flow in the air because Love took your breath away from what is ready for you out there.* Let that quick moment be a fragment in time as a memory of the past to enhance your emotional presence for preparation towards a Loving future.

So much memories in a time destined to be as life is the vision to see through the eyes of your heart as it was meant to be. Don't be fooled by those memories but let them be the magical key that opens the door to the future leaving the rest history. Allow your thoughts to guide you in the right path so you can follow the truth. Don't allow yourself to be misguided to a path with scattered up emotions blocking you from the right way to accidentally walk the wrong way. *Follow through your mind as it will lead you to where your heart takes you for a presence of Love to be true.* There is always an opening to the hole that will be filled with hope. *The type of person that will satisfy you to reach that emotional peak as the strength of your heart seeks to experience Love as an oriented belief.*

Learn to accept but never regret the life we chose as gifted as the next. We must cherish what's left in a world to accept. Full of joy and pain from the days passed; ending in flames if sins are real and not falsely named. Cool out and chill. Think hard about the game. The Love is driving you insane, steering you in the right direction and in the right lane. We have a job to do to help us regain the strength we obtain from our emotional strain. Not mix but fix the pieces from the gift of our Love interest as emotions tie the rift. Create that shift in thinking so quick for a reaction of guilt if you refuse to plea the fifth. Answer the questions asked by yourself to satisfy your mind so you do not need help.

Through the emotions you become delusional into believing that your heart is widely open even though your thoughts are broadly in motion towards the next step of true devotion. As a whole you must become deeply in tune with whomever is involved. Screeching and screaming inside for what is near which will result in a fatal flaw or an uprising roar. Turning back is difficult if your heart is pounding hard but the soft voice of your soul wants to fix the undone. *Beaming down from the sun with such heating flames as the desires strike life into the body of light creating obstacles to conquer a false sight.*

Turn back, rewind and fix all the regrets. A sense of remorse triggering the brain of intellect. The pain will intersect if the game is not met. Grasp all the power left. Allow your mind to manifest. Gather enough energy to collect and become in full effect. Overcoming the enslaved to become something brave with the sword of Love shining down from the heavens to the grave. Striking fear as engraved in the souls of the unmade. From yesterday to today, time has never been so vague. The universe is our slave as we journey through a maze of pain dreadfully not amazed by our superior ways of Love needed to end this emotional phase.

A long-lasting Love is learned from the orientation. Emotionally stable to handle deep thoughts about feelings from within. *Sharing is caring. Share those thoughts with your Love and care that was brought and painfully sought.* Piece the puzzle together in order to be clear minded towards your next step. *Organizing those feelings helps because they are scattered all over the place, splattered inside your face, consuming your brain and attempting to bring forth pain which must be controlled to handle what could be insane.*

Let your emotions free! They are trapped in a head that influences emotion with logic and sparks understanding with thought. *The true emotions need to be heard and thrown on the table. It is not good for them to be stored in the fridge and unstable.* They do spoil! *Never let your feelings and emotions go bad because they need to be fresh and ready to express.* You could have missed out on the opportunity of a lifetime if you don't let out how you feel. You are the One, a voice needs to be heard. Every word down to the tip needs to be said when it all comes down and emotionally drips to the way you feel. It is worth expressing once it's all out and spoken for instead of others guessing.

Emotional Orientation is the beginning of a deep compilation of true feelings from the heart and soul creating a sensation. Dig deep from within. Feel your heart racing. Feelings and emotions with no segregation. Understand what is felt in this deep consultation. Introduce emotions to the heart and start chasing what is truthfully in relation to your soul; the hole needed to be filled in duration. Break down the barrier that you're currently facing and freely explode in your own world of temptation.

True Passion

Feel fierce! Feel powerful! Feel the passion! *Use it towards your advantage to allow your heart to spit game. Win over shame to passionately gain what is true and honest to yourself about how you feel about someone else.* Let that someone know that you feel a certain way with such dominant swag and persistence as long as no boundaries are crossed and you are perceiving a level of respect that will result in a positive outcome no matter what the situation may hold. Relationship status is a major key factor when it comes down to the desire to grab what is wanted, even if deserved. *A certain level of respect needs to be addressed in order to impress and prevent a mess. Remember to feel the passion and start acting so you don't sit back to a negative reaction.*

Understand the truth; never lie and front. Keep it real and blunt. Show respect, control your anger and be ready to confront. The face in the mirror is your own so be ready to show passion through your heart because you need no help from anyone else. To act on pure instinct won't get you anywhere, you need to use True Passion as a tool towards heart fulfilled feelings to express in a respectful manner with your own unique swagger. *Learn to overcome the fear of rejection and a shy connection.* Speak your mind influenced from the heart powered by the soul.

Life as we know it is all based on the Will of God, we are all here for a reason to fulfill our purpose and reach our destiny. We all want everything precious we can get our hands on. Greed can only get you so far by putting yourself first when it comes to wanting almost everything. It is always believed to put others before yourself and for good karma, but in the end, there must be times when You have to be #1 and not the person in front of you. The choice is always in the eyes of the beholder.

Life is a like a Lincoln MKS. We use power, motion and speed to accelerate our full-size luxury body with twin-turbo ideas through automatic brain transmission. We are a big lean speeding machine when it comes to daily routines, activities, hobbies, work and keeping occupied. Embrace passionate instincts to take control and enhance your actions to achieve more than the believable.

Explosion, erosion and mentally frozen. Time to start loading what is known and what is chosen. From the heart cracking the brain's coding to widely open the door to Love as it's molding. Forming and spiritually storming from the inside pouring hot desire, melting and soaring through the passion as it's roaring; shocking the heart to wake up and stop snoring.

Act on how you feel. Perform what's real as True Passion runs through the door leading you to a good deal. A deal solid and gold as emotions become bold. It is time to be true and only to you. If your heart is burning desire, allow sincerity to unlock the truth. Take charge of who you are and what's holding you back from becoming You. *Accept it and never reject it. A good opportunity in life doesn't come too often. Take complete advantage of a reward as it's walking. They go by fast so catch it, keep it, hold on, never release it. When you perform on pure emotion in a respectful way, you will believe it.* Become brave and become a living proof.

Passion found; ready and bound from time and around with truth from the sound. Hear the emotion through the heart of a hound. Aggressive and profound, this is the big rebound.

The only truth to find is the truth in yourself. When you strongly believe in something you should trust that instinct and go for broke! Whether possible or not, the True Passion in belief strives you to do more and go in for the kill! *Follow what you believe in and be ready to start achieving!*

Believe, achieve, what's up your sleeve? Don't be naive. Never deceive but only relieve the stress from inside that is planting a seed that you must foresee in order to live a success without grieve.

There are billions of people and respect is always the key to anything good as it all should be. No one wants to feel disrespected, hear anything disrespectful or see anything disrespectful. *Show respect and there will be no regrets. Anything can be possible as long as things are done respectfully. Follow your heart as it beats correctively to achieve everything successfully. Positive action must take place for true possibilities to come true. Success becomes more important than anything because the future is closing in on you.* Respect control and control passion. Control your actions so that passion can lead to success.

When you want something just go for it. It can't hurt if what you want isn't some devilish act but a strong desire of good. The same passion in which you use for the unnecessary things should be used for the things that you desire the most. *Treat yourself. You don't need help. Make it happen in front of everyone else.* You have your own mind, use it, think about what feels right and think about what is right. *The things you want bad in life at times may feel so far away but we are here to live another day. The desire, the passion and hunger. Such a drive is what keeps you alive.*

The hunger, the thunder from deep down under. The power you have hits you hard enough to wonder. Don't be blind. Deep undercover from the mind; an inside job from developing a Lover that's been hidden from sight to a positive find.

Positivity is a major factor in Love and True Passion. It is the key for the doors that block emotions and passionate movements. Unlock those doors and you move on passed the obstacles that were once in your way. *It's time to throw all that negativity away. Use positivity as fuel for passion to stay and bring success and Love to live life the next day.*

Passionate moments are there, use as much energy in you as can be without draining yourself down. Feel the sensation when an urge to achieve something shocks you and wakes you up a little more. Get that new job you've been hunting for, get that girl you've been hunting for, or even get that Thanksgiving turkey you've been hunting for. The hunt is on! Passionately and desirably, a Love is there as a guideline for successful results.

Compassion, action and reaction in fashion resulting in satisfaction. As time is cut down to a fraction mathematically inaction through numbers to attraction in one boiled up caption. The word Love was made through True Passion.

CORE PERSONALITY

Core Personality

The core is the center of everything. Once you get to the middle of what's going on, a bigger understanding will come in effect. The center of anything will benefit your mind to get to the bottom of things and reach the answers faster. When it comes down to the Core Personality, we are talking about some real deep stuff right here. Everyone is different due to their personality. The Core Personality emphasizes the truth behind who you really are. To know the true colors of a person and how they really are will answer many questions that you have to figure out about your very own emotions and where you stand.

To reach the center of Love requires a Core Personality. *The will to get to know someone enhances the chance to advance and find Love and romance.* Being social and keeping it real are the aspects of a Core Personality to address conversation in a nice manner. It is scary to live in a false reality and be caught up in what's real and what's fake. *The truth is what we seek for, the answers are what we reach for.* Get to know as much as you can about someone that can be a possible future Love. Everything about them represents the truth. Ask and you shall receive through conversation. The real deal lies within words spoken from the heart, throughout the brain and influenced by the spirit.

It really takes a lifetime to get to know a person. In the beginning you will know the most about a person in a short amount of time supposedly due to the will to want to know more about a stranger. As the years pass you will learn more about that former stranger and eventually refresh on the things in the beginning conversations with that person. It's an ongoing cycle that will continue as long as that will has not gone away.

What's real? What's fake? So much to intake. Time to elaborate to figure out what's great. The other side of the gate explains the truth to what's fate.

React to how you act and be exact to the fact. It is said that Love is blind, but it really is just hard to find. The fact that you act a certain way is because you feel something. Sometimes that something can lead into Love or actually is Love at its beginning stage. *It is not complicated with the way you feel. It is complicated to figure out what's real.*

Emotions tower the spirit and create an interaction between the mind and heart traction to form emotion as a fraction multiplying satisfaction with such aggressive action on a feeling-based attraction.

Present Love as it is money paid instead of only getting laid so that your heart cannot fade but only upgrade to reach the light behind the shade. Feels so good to surpass all the rage; emotionally brave to begin what's made. A romance to engrave for your heart to shock the mind and come out from behind. We are not trapped in time; with Love to hustle and grind to find what's rightfully fine.

How many licks does it take to get to the center of a tootsie pop? The world may never know. This is just a metaphor for getting to the center of Love. When will I get there? How long will I stay there? How do I not leave? All these questions will run through your head if you want a Love that is strong and want to keep it that way.

With questions to ask and answers to hide, there is a door that unlocks the lies. To find the truth so that you now can enter, all the emotions from the center. Never fall into a trap. Become the preventer, the hero, the savior and the Love documenter.

Let's talk about super powers, let's talk about reading minds. A clear example brought to our attention was NBC's hit TV show "Heroes". Imagine having the character Matt Parkman's power to read minds. There would be nothing but the truth because you would know when someone is lying to you. You can know a person before actually knowing a person just by reading their thoughts. You can technically cheat your way to Love with these new powers but the best way to use them should assist you to know the truth so that you don't waste time and don't get played. You will discover the core to everyone's personality.

Living in the first century of the 3rd millennium is a different era from when our grandparents were our age. The 21st century is a new age for technology and a different world of Love. We need to learn from the Love of our elders and become inspired to draw our passion out and create Love as it was meant to be. *Inspire others to reveal their true self rather than just intercourse and wealth.* The core of ourselves is what needs to be brought out instead of technology itself taking over. In the 20th century, at one point there were no TVs, no cell phones and no computers. Imagine a world without that stuff. All that you have is yourself. Communication took over the world and allowed people to actually get to know one another rather than the drama of television and social media. *One on one and face to face. That was a time when Love was great. Let's rewind and bring those elements back to our time and capture the core of what we find.*

Getting down to the core means to get down to the nitty gritty; to know the truth. Everyone should want to get to the bottom of things so that you are well aware of what is actually going on and not being misled into a fantasy. At times it can't hurt to live in the now, but it can hurt to find out that everything wasn't what it seemed and was one big lie. *Honest conversations with deep observations show meaningful relations towards building a true foundation.*

Understand the truth behind personality as a whole because the goal is to know everything about the soul. We are an entity shielded by a body that fuses the mind, heart and soul as one creating who we are through the vision of eyes.

Disguised to explore life as created by God to observe the world through our newly eyes. Waiting to one day fly freely as energy along the skies with the ones we have missed. Serving God as angels in heavenly bliss and watching over the world as a spiritual mist.

Core Personality, smart mentality. Deep sexuality, our actuality. This is life, this is reality. As we grow up gradually and surpass all the agony to express ourselves naturally and emphasize vitality to overpower fatalities. This is Love forming as it should be. Feels like an opinion made factually.

FALSE TRUTH

Chapter 10

False Truth

Life as we know it may only be a fragment of our own imagination. It has been known that the mind plays tricks on us. We can be hypnotized into believing a False Truth created in our own mind. We can be fooled into acting like a dog at the sound of a bell or mentally convinced that a feather weighs a ton. That right there is brain power, the energy influenced by the mind and perceived as a False Truth.

It is scary to know that our own dreams can kill us. We can be convinced by our own very dream that we are drowning and literally suffocate in our own sleep in reality. Dreams can be a blessing and a curse. Let's not let fear take control but use fear as energy fueling us to overcome psychological projections. We need to take advantage of what's not real and enhance our own dreams with our own positive influences in order to rid the brain of all danger that lurks from within. Remember, Freddy Krueger doesn't exist!

It can be believed that Love doesn't exist and that we are tricked to believe that lust represents emotion and that when you are aroused you have feelings. We cannot be convinced by a False Truth to lead us in the wrong direction. *It's all about connection, affection, we should stop guessing. Allow Love to become a reality and stop stressing. Take control and do not allow in any false assets. Hypnosis and dreams must be controlled and influenced by positivity so that we can never accidentally let in negativity. For that the bad things can happen if we do not step up to be a hero and fight for what's right and not wrong in sight.* We must do our best to positively inspire our own fantasies to become adventures and feel like a movie or story with a happy ending. Let fantasies come true in the most possible way as can be not defying reality in physics. *The truth can be told for what it may hold and kept to ourselves to be stored, shared, but never sold.*

To dream it may seem to light as a beam. It strikes with all might and blinds us of all sight. With closed eyes we might daze and sleep deep with no light. So tense and so tight as we believe what may be right, but we dream to fly great heights. It may seem so right that we are roaming each day as we sleep through the night. We get hypnotized by fiction memorized as we lie behind our very eyes and are convinced for what it hides; hidden within what ties in. As in life we begin. We dream to believe in, but we must understand realism from what we are really facing and see reality as a fairytale dreamed to have that happy ending.

Believe what is known to be possible in the zone. As we progress on our own to enlighten what feels alone. Help out those who are trapped in their very own twilight zone. Living with themselves; stuck in the flames of their very own hell. It's time to work as one and tell your story well. Released from hiding in a shell slow paced you can tell living on a flat world where you almost fell.

Imagine living in "The Matrix", a world that appears more real than the world you are already living in. Imagine at this very moment we are living in a dream, and when we dream it is within a dream on the verge of "Inception" to figure out the truth behind an idea that may not be true. Our memory can be vanished and we are living in our own "Total Recall" or even dream for the day of controlling our very own "Avatar" to enhance life altering the truth as humanity knows it. In the end this may all be foolish talk but real or not it is Love that makes you understand the realism of your life. Living in a fake world is just adolescence behind the life we live in.

Distinguish what's real and fake to decide your fate to find Love passed the hate. In a world of the great where evil interferes and sets in gear to prepare for the fear of the death that is near.

We must work as a team, prevent the evil from infecting our minds to believe a False Truth that can destroy our own heart and slowly demolish our soul. Use all the positive energy you got to resolve the issue on the spot. *Don't be fooled by the Freddy Kruegers in dreams as we are mentally losing or the David Blaines in illusions for what is real is what we're choosing.*

The insanity of losing your mind will bite you from behind as you struggle to find the truth hidden through signs. The very signs that influence people to assume many things that may shine some light or lose all sight. The wrong and the right is what creates the fight that we are eager to win. Take the world for a spin as time passes by, we must look and watch the world as a clock with time we can tell what is heaven and what is hell.

Reality or a dream? Believe what is real but sometimes what is real you wish were dreams. Dreams being real isn't the reality of it all. What is real is living the dream. Something so real that may feel like a happy ending or a terrible nightmare. Accept it for what it is.

The positivity dreams bring will be inspiring as life sings to connect everything together to make wonderful things because the only thing that makes you sane is the joy conquering over the pain.

Live the life you want; live the life you choose but remember what makes you human and what it means to live in someone else's shoes. The truth hurts but you still want it because it is better to know than better to live life as a question. There are too many questions we already have as it is. Let's live to search for answers and make decisions based on the truth rather than based on assumption. *It is always bad to assume because the truth is always hidden beyond the lies that are presumed.* Living with lies makes you have stuff you want to get off your chest. *When you let it all out, the truth sets you free and clear for what the next step should be.*

Trapped in the mind; believing a False Truth is what should be vanished, gone, then poof! Creating a chain, a cycling loop that strikes from behind to force you back in reality just in time to pursue and make progress towards the future You.

KNOWLEDGEABLE BEAUTY

Chapter 11

Knowledgeable Beauty

It has been said that beauty lies behind the eyes of the beholder. *Beauty itself has been mesmerized by the eyes from those who realize attraction as a spectacle created from the inside.* Thoughts from the mind are stimulated by the nerves to arouse sensational feelings in the stomach, filling the body with butterflies and deepness felt as a possible beginning stage towards creating Love. *A Love to answer a false truth that will endure a core personality causing an effect to reflect what is known to cleanse and eject.* A fresh start towards possibly finding a destined Love is there and the present presents presentation towards the future which is happening right now and not slowing down. *Keep up and show who really is tough!*

Knowledge is power. Love is sour. Everyday hearts are broken by the hour. Sexy and hot is what confuses the mind into lust rather than an honest Love. *It is hard to control what is not known, but we are in our zone and can focus on our own to figure out what is really known.* To know is based on knowledge and to Love is based on emotion. *Allow what is felt to stumble through and rumble within to formulate emotion as its own feeling.* Wake up and take in what it brings.

Knowledge is very important when it comes to beauty because you need to be able to understand what beauty really means. Experience will grow as you evolve from a child to an adult. What you feel through attraction and adrenaline will encourage your heart to know what beauty really means once you learn the core to feelings and emotions. Don't be afraid of what you are feeling because that feeling alone is a blessing in itself. Sometimes you will be given a second to cleanse the sins for a change towards a better future. Even if pure good exists within that person, their day will come.

There is an equal, a sequel to good and bad people. An upgrade in life with Love to overcome evil. Straight from the past, the present holds the prequel towards a new life to live and a future that is meaningful.

Everyone is beautiful in their own unique way whether we realize it or not. Personality sometimes overshadows attraction and can build an unexpected attraction. Everyone may find beauty in different people, not everyone will agree with the rating of an appearance on a scale from 1 to 10. Everyone's mind stimulates attraction differently and once you actually get to know a person the stimulation can actually change. Now don't get me wrong, there will be many people out there that we see the beauty in. The question is who is the one that is destined?

As we grow up we progress and understand what it means when a female is called beautiful or a man is called handsome. As a kid you will discover cute, as a teenager you will discover sexy and as an adult you will discover what connection means. It is bigger than raw attraction alone even when we feel aroused. Trust, loyalty and other qualities within a personality may draw us towards beauty in a new way and only add to the physical attraction that already is there.

We are who we are based on our morality inspired by our guardians. Our neighborhood and surroundings impact our judgement which influences our very own personality. The decisions we make are all based on our logic. The way we were raised, the ones who influenced us and inspired us in a good or bad way have the biggest impact on how we all act. A personality develops and our understanding on beauty alone is based off of that knowledge and how we feel on the inside.

From beauty to the beast, we live to say the least making our hearts beat from childhood tales growing into new feet. Living life with a better understanding of the stories that made us breathe through fantasy into reality to create our very own normality.

Triple Ls (Love, Laugh, Live) is what it's all about. To Love gives meaning to life, to laugh brings joy to life and to live allows you to have a life. Represent the Will of God and understand everything as it happens and why we are here exactly, smack on this Earth. There is a reason for everything and everything has its purpose. Understanding reality through all of its aspects that will benefit a better result in future living all destined for success and Love.

Have the knowledge to remember. Battle beauty, TKO, contender. Body real tight, so perfect, so slender. Hungry for Love, so juicy and so tender. There is pressure to find the pleasure. Finding the right one is a journey and adventure. Got it in the bag, attraction, danger. Money, power, respect. This stuff is real major. Passing through time with Love on a hanger. Hold it real tight. A future beauty to remember.

Never forget the feelings you won't regret because a preparation for True Love will already be in motion and set. Past relationships and emotions only prepare you for the real deal, a future ahead of you. *Don't be an emotional wreck. Just chill, relax and be ready for the next step. Go and spit that game without any emotional pain.* Remain confident and always stay ahead of the game because there will be tough situations to come and must be dealt with. "That's the way Love goes" as Janet Jackson once sang reflects on the statement "it is what it is". *We can't control what comes and what goes. Love will shine brightly over our toes as we compose feelings in our heart for what it shows. Allow our emotions to grow.*

Beauty is the heart of mind. Feeling an attraction for the wonderful sight right in front of you is a good feeling and a different feeling from just seeing a nice view on a rooftop. *When you feel attraction, you physically are in action.* True attraction comes from not only that but also emotional bondage and spiritual connection. *It's time to connect and recollect how you feel about finding out if a Love can be emotionally real.*

Knowledgeable Beauty can be established real newly behind the eyes of the beholder who may act real boozy. But it's really the emotions getting all woozy in a heartfelt dimension to find out who it should be. The One; the gun; a shot of Love. Do not run. With weight on the shoulders feeling like a ton, emotionally stunned and the day is done. Feelings have begun with power from each one holding its own beam of light. Within the dark night there's limited sight to fight through the dark to make sense of what's right.

Chapter *12*

Twilight Zone

You are now entering the zone, the Twilight Zone where Vampires, Werewolves and other worldly phenomena exist. *Journey through a world where "seeing is believing" and the unreal is deceiving. Magical powers floating around can be misleading.* It is time to channel your energy and prepare yourself for the ride of a lifetime. Sit back and enjoy the ride in the never-ending roller coaster headed into a world of illusion and darkness.

We all have a dark side to us, some of us have it locked away and cannot seem to find the key, others found the key and choose when to use it and others can't seem to find the lock. As we grow, we learn about self-control and as we learn how to control, we figure out what to control. Our mentality is there for a reason and to give us the opportunity to control our very own lives. It is up to us to control it in an orderly fashioned manner with respect and honesty to make everything right.

"The Twilight Zone" the TV show is a series of unrelated stories that contain drama, psychological thriller, fantasy, science fiction, suspense with a little horror usually concluding with an unexpected twist. That actually can relate to Love in its own twisted way. All of those elements are the trials and tribulations of a relationship.

Love may be found in the strangest ways. The tale seems similar when you watch movies and shows such as "Twilight" and "True Blood". The concept is similar with the girl falling in Love with the vampire. Love comes in mysterious ways, even such in "Beauty and the Beast" which is another concept of True Love. Your soul is what stimulates deep feelings in the 1st place even if you find someone physically attractive. If you are truly in Love with them then it is their Soul in which you Love. Their Soul represents the truth which overshadows physicality itself by emotion set in motion.

Always cherish the ones, especially the One that you Love for that Love is supposed to be magical in its own sense especially when feelings and emotions are in action. *When it comes down to reality, Love it or not, a real Love is there for you to spot.* Show affection to family and especially your partner no matter who or what they are. Don't get caught up living in the Twilight Zone, get caught up being in the zone and use fictional Love aspects towards a real and True Love that exists in our reality.

Goblins, ghouls, zombies, ghosts, don't be afraid of spiritual hosts. Live to overcome every fictional hoax. Live life without fear, no overdose. Hold on to memories of who we Love the most. No Boogeyman can attack our souls if we are tied with Love that fills all holes. As long as we fly high in the sky. As long as we live like we never died. No blood sucker can hypnotize our minds if you find a Love that is not blind. An illusion to live is forgetful to give. Live life to the fullest and make it big!

No matter how you feel, never wish to be a superhero, vampire or God because:

1) We can't
2) We contain the opportunity to use our heart more than anything because we are human
3) We are not immortal; therefore, we have something to live for
4) We don't have to risk causing mayhem with supernatural powers

We are blessed to be human due to the fact that we contain the most passion, compassion and satisfaction towards Love and success. *It is our job to live a healthy lifestyle of good measure and breathe fresh air in a world filled with fun, excitement and adventure! Love who you are and remember we are not vampires or Avengers. We are humans emotionally linked together!*

Imagine living in a world of "The Walking Dead" where everyone around you are mindless walkers and finding a living person that you can trust is very difficult. As brutal as the walkers may seem, the untrustworthy people are just as worse. Survival is the key, you will fight against being bitten, stabbed or shot at. In our reality it is almost the same thing as far as trust is concerned. Without trust there is nothing. Relationships wouldn't work, Love wouldn't exist and the future would be fatal. No matter what kind of world we live in trust will always be a key factor in bringing Love to life. We must all learn to trust but be extremely cautious while doing so. Never follow the saying, "Don't trust no one" because we still need that amenity in life to move forward in Love and success. *Escaping in our fantasy world isn't a bad thing but trusting someone is nothing more than a real thing.*

Sometimes we tend to venture out in our own fantasy world which may perceive the notion of a quick escape from reality. Those escapes allow us to vision things we wish to happen or can't happen. Love really doesn't exist in the fantasy realm but may trigger a confident action towards finding it or at least keeping it. *The influence from fictional shows, movies, comics and books may impact the mind to react accordingly. Actions taken are not what they are normally only because the results never end up perfectly.*

We live to seek one mile ahead to take that leap. We journey through many adventures in our dreams and reality and those experiences make us realize how precious life really is. In disaster films such as "The Day After Tomorrow", "War of the Worlds", "2012" and "San Andreas" there are classic examples of destructive events that usually end in the main character surviving. We are the main character and the impossible became achievable. Even when you have a dream that feels like a movie or get that unfortunate rare opportunity to survive a catastrophe, you will then realize how short life seems to be and usually want Love by your side from that day forward.

Welcome to the Twilight Zone where things are not known, trapped in a parallel world to make it on your own. Feels like you are alone, you hear vivid deep moans. Mentally insane with evil eyes and foam. Strange and deranged to feel right at home. Feel the lively tone as we start over and revive, we feel so alive. With confidence we strive to go head first as we dive for that aggressive drive to fight to survive in the Twilight Zone. Passed midnight, as we sleep through the night, we wake up to the sight of a world real bright. Prepare for lift off, it's time to take flight and wake up to see the light.

Chapter 13

Death

To die or not to die, that is the question. (To come at the world straight forward) Unfortunately we die, and not even by choice. To lighten things up a bit, we die because if we don't then the world will be way too overpopulated. Imagine living in a world where you wake up to 10 people in your bed and go to the bathroom with 5 people staring at you. That would be an extremely awkward and uncomfortable world to live in, don't you think. We live on the planet Earth which is round meaning it connects. There is no never-ending trail, eventually you will end up right where you started from. There needs to be space in order to breathe and actually grasp a moment to think. The logic behind it all is so everybody can live comfortably enough to create a future where humans still exists.

As we journey back in time when the world appeared to be flat due to the lack of technology at that time, it was a very different place where people thought differently. To finally learn that the shape of the planet you live in is really round is the blow to the head. Now you then know that everything is connected and falling off the edge to your death is not an option. *As time passes by you then begin to realize that diseases and plagues take over the world which may seem so vague.* Sickness begins to spread as a new way dying may defy the belief in that era. We then realize how precious life really is and that we can't control the dominant force known as Time. The reality is that our time clock is ticking and as a living breathing human being, we must make the most of our life in this world.

On television, the news shows you the harsh reality of Death in today's society. On the flip side, movies and shows portray Death in sometimes a comedic way to lighten up the mood. Even though there is really nothing good about it we must remain positive and happy in the life we live so that when that time comes, we accept it and live on.

The purpose of After Life may appear to be closer with God, become one of his Guardians (Angels). We will then reconnect with Loved ones once lost in the past both human and animal, and just to see them again will feel amazing. Imagine just floating around the universe as spiritual energy not ever having to worry about any form of pain ever again. Now that doesn't sound bad at all. Living as a breathing soul within a body allows us to live a life in a different way and may possibly prepare us to even become future Angels (Guardians). We live this life for the will of God and for ourselves. To experience fun adventurous activities, family-oriented Love, emotional conversation and sexual encounters are all part of what we are here for. We live to reach destiny and it might be different from others but True Love may seem like a really good reason to want to live you know.

Live towards the future destiny and receive Love as the rest should be. Time's flying on the money tree on land where the Love should be. Bloodshed and violent rivalries instead of living peacefully should not be the case literally. We need to fight evil with Love globally and live to start a family. The end is near it may seem to be. Prevent the loss of possibility to complete life as it's destined to be and live to Love for the sake of humanity.

No one wants to die. The cycle of life grows real high, as we live for the future we pray to the heavens in the sky to survive a long life and hope to never say goodbye. All we do is hear about deaths every day, but at the same time, we always hear about new births. That's what makes the world go around, death and birth. When one dies, another one is born. It almost makes you think about the possibility of reincarnation. Now it does make sense. It also makes you think about having more than one life with the memory erased from the other. There are people out there that mistake thoughts, dreams and visions with actual past memories. Imagine if those memories were from a prior life? Just a food for thought, good to know and think about. *The many possibilities in life seem glorious. Death seems notorious but we make the best of more to us and live to have Love as a creation towards success to make a floor for us. Cradle to the grave, live your life young and brave.*

Never allow yourself to think about dying because if you say everything is ok then you would be lying. Disguising your emotions may allow others to feel good but once the negative energy is absorbed by others then your cover is blown. It is best to be honest about what you're feeling because you never know if that random person or someone close you know gives you the advice you seek for.

Fans of WWE Superstar John Cena chant "Let's go Cena, Cena sucks!". Love him or not but he always goes by the quote "Never give up". When times are rough and we tend to allow negativity in we must follow that quote because it is too easy to give up. Life is not easy. To some it is not easy to live. Let us become inspired by the ones who know how to live and inspire the people who find it hard. We control our lives and make it worth living.

From the unknown to the known, live to Love and find it on your own. Time is flying fast alone. Think really fast and really grown. We are roaming the world with thoughts forgetting where is home. In a world where pain is alive and shown, Love is the bullet; Death is not. Show no fear towards what you got. Make a statement save a spot reserved for Love rising high yet hot. Burn away Death to live a lot with God and Love as an eternal day that shines bright, washing the pain away.

THIS CHAPTER SHOULD NOT BE ENCOURAGING TO DIE OR COMMIT SUICIDE BASED ON AFTER LIFE OR HAVING NOTHING TO LIVE FOR. YOU ARE HERE ON THIS PLANET FOR A REASON AND HAVE A GOD GIVEN PURPOSE WHICH YOU WILL REALIZE AT SOME POINT IN YOUR LIFE. YOU SHOULD REALIZE DEATH MORE AS A NATURAL PART OF LIFE RATHER THAN A FORCEFUL PART OF LIFE. NEVER FORGET WHO YOU ARE AND REACH FOR THE STARS. BECOME SUCCESSFUL AND ALLOW LOVE TO CONSUME YOU. LIVE LIFE TO THE FULLEST AND DIE NATURALLY.

Chapter 14

Connection

As referenced on FOX's TV series "Touch", we are all connected. Everybody and everything in this world are connected with numbers, shapes and patterns. The thing is that we don't realize it. Every little thing counts. People in life that we cross paths with happen for a reason. They can be a person who passed by in the past and unknowingly reuinite in the future.

Pinpoint all the dots together by recollecting every small thing that happened in a day, week and even a month. Connect everything together to understand the connection of events and especially people which impact your future.

The future is near. What direction do we steer? As we drive through life, we learn what is far and what is near. Given the time or place, we impact the world unknowingly in fear of making the wrong choice for the Love that is hiding but still is here. Karma is a beast that will infest minds and hurt ears if we don't respect a life of Love that we must learn and must hear. Wake up and shine bright to see the world crystal clear.

Pray for a good future because our actions create it even though the one almighty already knows. We must follow the yellow brick road to reach Oz which we can consider as God except it's not fake. We meet the people we connect with on that path that guides us to the end where we become happy and successful. Remember that only God knows all the answers there is. We are here on this Earth to seek those answers out to fulfill the voids missing in order to better ourselves for enhancement towards the future ahead that we strive to live for.

The connection between family is known due to the handy downs of traits. All the traits get passed down in sync with the development of new traits to create a unique individual. It's what makes everyone different yet the same. We are a fusion of our mother and father. We even carry some traits from grandparents and possibly aunts and uncles too. *It's what makes us who we are and so unique from afar.* Personality and appearance distinguish one from another even with identical twins there is one slight blemish that separates the two. In the end it is your personality that is a big part of who you are. The influences from culture, lively hood and who's around you definitely impact personality to the core. You already are you and must become a leader not a follower so that people follow you and are inspired enough to transform into a future leader.

Everything whether we realize it or not is connected, selected, thoroughly respected. Hate it or Love it the choice is selective. We journey through life to progress and be directed. We really need to take charge and be a little more directive in the decisions we make and the goals we elected. A future to live is a future invested!

Our future revolves around being successful and inspiring ours to become successful, that is how we connect with the world. Nobody is perfect and everyone does not know everything.

As shown in the film "Reach Me", a diverse group of people are united by a powerful book published by an unknown mysterious author. When the book's positive message goes viral, a hip-hop mogul, an undercover cop, a struggling actress, a pair of hit men, a former inmate and a journalist and his editor are inspired to change their lives by facing their own fears. Those fears connect them and draw them together.

Connections can go as deep as Hannibal and Clarice where the psychological mindset leads them to have a strange bond with one another just based off the strong connection they had from the beginning. Even the most sadistic people can connect with the most innocent. It's always something about that person that draws them together.

Rivalry and savagery boil up emotions silently, leading to acts of Love violently, ending up in irony to what may appear rightfully in the mind of someone who acts privately.

Everyone acts differently and has their own way of portraying themselves to others and expressing how they feel. People come and people go but the chosen are the ones who connect the outcome to the problems dealt with at present times.

As we journey through the valley of the shadow of death, we begin to realize how important life really is and that fear itself is just an obstacle that we must cross to move on. All those obstacles we face are shared with others and that is why the Connection is so strong between us and the world. Never forget that there is always someone else out there dealing with the same situation we are. Don't set barriers in your way, allow others in so that you can understand who they really are and their importance to us and impact that they have on the world.

Let's metaphorically perceive the board game "Connect 4" as humans. So, we got the red dots and black dots. Let's think of them as two different families or two different groups of friends. So, the idea is to connect four red dots or four black dots together in order to win. In life we know or unknowingly choose those who are right for us to be a friend or have in our life. Sometimes even a stranger may cross paths and somehow become connected to a situation you are going through at that very moment. Well God is playing Heavenly Connect 4 and connecting us all together and not necessarily four but a good amount needed to be connected to actually create our predetermined future. *Only time will tell but if we connect the dots together, we will be better than ever.*

The Connection to Love will leave you at awe, raw, straight to the core, no regrets and left with no withdraw. Avenge a heartbreak that you never saw by accepting and connecting the wrong you are correcting, thoroughly respecting as an insight towards rejection. Allow what is known to guide you in the right direction towards a victory, liberty with heavy artillery. Avoid all the misery through an emotional roller coaster leading to an epiphany so you can understand True Love as a journey through a trilogy.

Chapter 15

Live Beyond

What does it mean to Live Beyond? Live Beyond what? Live Beyond who? Well it may seem as if it obviously means beyond life on Earth, which it does. But just think about living passed the life we already have, reconnected with long lost Loved ones and exploring the universe in a new way. We must cherish every moment of the life we already live and prepare ourselves for the next one. If we genuinely are good people, we might just be rewarded with the opportunity to become an Angel, one of God's Guardians. It's like joining the army in heaven, a pretty cool logic.

As shown in the movie "Legion", the main character who helps fight off the demons encounters the sacrifice of one of the Angels. After the Angel dies then he starts to transform into an Angel. The throne has been passed on, a gift has been given, a new savior has arrived!

Imagine living your whole life to know that there is more to live for and that all the memories from this life only impact the next one. Never live with regrets because the future revolves around the present. To live with the "what ifs" only get in the way for what is next. Stop living in the past and start understanding the present so that you can start living towards the future. Move forward, not backwards. If there is a life to Live Beyond then live this life right so that the next one will be even better. Most of us deserve to be rewarded. Let's be rewarded with the gift to Live Beyond, but in the best way possibly. Do Not! And I repeat Do Not mess up your life and live in hell. That definitely does not seem like a good place to live at all! *Live right and see the light!*

There are some shows on the TV channel BIO such as "Ghost Adventures" which show the latest EMF meters as they actually speak words to you recorded from paranormal sounds spoken from spirits. To hear such words and names that describe legitimate facts show the clear proof of life after death. Even all the stories of near-death experiences which describe what is seen through the passing process between life and death make you really consider it being a reality.

To wonder, thunder, storms with such hunger. Joy is the prey; anger is the hunter. Don't live through life where you are stuck deep down under. Rise to the top, be faster than a roadrunner, close range like a top gunner, so insane you almost wondered why you are thinking of the next life before this one is even over.

Even though there is no real proof that all the public knows about life beyond, we must explore that possibility. It is said that seeing is believing and in most cases that is true. Once you see something with your very own eyes then you know what you are seeing is real and not fake. The belief of hallucinations may overcome what may seem hard to believe. Examples of that are on truTV's "The Carbonaro Effect". An example of a skit shown was two paintings and one was a barn and the other was a group of people. Initially there was a horse in a stable, next thing you know it the horse appears in the other painting with the people and the stable is empty. The person thought they were just seeing things. This is just one skit of many when people found it hard to believe what they were seeing right in front of them.

Now to get a bit deeper into things, imagine living the life, imagine living as a king/queen where you are on top and can literally see it all and buy it all. The only problem is that you can't get with them all or at least the one you really want. Money can only buy so much. *Showing people the real you will let them know what is really true.* Let the truth be told in a world full of lies, betrayal and lust. You can have all the money in the world but without Love you are nothing! Success can only last you so far. Now some people may be fine without it and live a life hassle free with no commitment. They just don't know what they are missing out on when you get to feel real emotions towards someone you truly Love, whether it be a significant other or your very own child. That Love will hit you hard even if you are the toughest S.O.B. alive. *Don't be afraid to let Love in. Accept change as a new beginning.*

Nice to meet you. How you doing? Is this the one that you are choosing? Is this what you want to be pursuing? Are you winning or are you losing? Love is blind, open your eyes and start seeing. This is air that you are breathing. Find the one for you to plant the seed in. This is the life you should be experiencing. This is greatness, start achieving!

The human mind can think so far ahead that you might forget the more important things instead. Live to Love as Love will be given and said for the life that we live contains meaning tied together like thread. We are all here for significance and experience. Enjoy all the fun times shared over the times later rewarded as gifts for all the hard work accomplished.

Follow through your heart and Live Beyond the hope. The faith given to you from the heavens above will guide you in the direction which is needed. The pathway in the spiritual realm is sitting there waiting for you. *Allow your soulful energy to take action for the true satisfaction.* Start living for once and remember why you are here and what your purpose is. Follow this statement quoted by Big E from New Day in WWE: "Don't you dare be sour! Embrace the New Day and feel the Power!"

Remember that anything is possible. Achieve the improvable! Live the longest life as can be and never let go of Love. Take Love onto the next life because it is that Love that makes this life meaningful and that Love that will create truth in living forever as a God made spiritual entitiy with Love as a companion to watch over your very own descendents built for the future that we are crafted as an eternal essence collecting all of the blessings!

Live Beyond life and Live Beyond the truth. We have a long life to live as we journey for the proof of a Love surpassed a day. Days pass away and years will always stay. Memories from many days prepare us for that day when we rejoice and we pray. We make it on the way towards a lasting Love endlessly every day.

FINDING THE ONE

Chapter 16

Finding the One

Many ask and many may wonder, who is the One? Does the One really exist? Is there really even a One? Well, in order to make Two you need One and it is the One's job to add to You for the start of a relationship for Two. *Togetherness is the answer and the One fills in all the blanks, solving all problems, providing Love and nothing but thanks.*

To really fall in deep Love with someone that endlessly provides you with nothing but care and support the whole way through, Loves you and molds you into everything rightfully true represents nothing more but the One for You.

This is really simple and effective knowing that there is a One out there for everybody. *Not everyone can find them but somewhere far or somewhere close, the One is out there waiting for Love just like you willingly the most.*

Finding the One is like finding buried treasure of the unknown deep under the sea, a needle in a haystack or simply winning the lottery. In terms of Disney's Aladdin, there is a magic lamp that summons a genie who grants 3 wishes. Unfortunately, we don't know of any magic lamps or any genies, but what we can do is make 3 wishes and pray that they come true. We rely on hope and chance for such faith to exist. *Stay positive and remain confident that our day will come if it hasn't come yet in Finding the One.*

Is there Love? And if so where? You can dream for something rare. You can feel it in the air that there is someone way out there that gives your heart joy and care to find Love in a world that appears unfair. We live to stay alive with nothing to bear as painlessly as can be with truth or dare to make things happen loud and clear for what is near to come right here. No questions asked as we shift gear for a more confident outlook on Love existing in a new world with less fear.

Act brave and become fearless because the obstacles that await you will consume your spirit. Become "The Man Without Fear", become the Daredevil. Blind, yet your remaining four senses function with superhuman accuracy and sensitivity, giving you abilities far beyond the limits of a sighted person. Life would be in the dark blending in with the darkness that is in this world. *Find that One that will assist you in your journey to your very own fate. Lead to a light that can shine above hate and become something great.*

Journey through "The Matrix". Imagine if you are the One like Neo. Learn the truth and become drawn into a rebellion against the machines, which involves other people who have been freed from the "dream world". In those terms, technology represents the machines because it is growing so fast as these years continue to pass by. The "dream world" can be represented as unfortunate as the world we live in. Free your mind from all the negative walls that block us from the doors waiting to be unlocked. *We struggle through the weak and our true potential is what we seek. Allow yourself to grow even stronger, allow yourself to dream even bigger and allow yourself to become a winner!*

Unfortunately, in this world not everyone finds the One. There literally are people that are in a happy relationship and then 10 years later it's over! That's crazy! 10 years living delusional in an illusion of Love yet that person was never the One to begin with. It makes you think what really is out there and who is the One for you if they even do exist. *As unfortunate as it may seem, we must stay confident to live the dream.* Live up to God's expectations on peace and happiness visualized as the perfect world even though it is not the world we live in. The more people that aim for perfection, the closer we will be to a perfect world even though it doesn't exist.

Make things happen and become the captain of your very own ship that you appear to be trapped in. Time to take action so that you do not sink. Survive the brink of destruction that makes us link.

You will meet many people in your life. *One out of the many may be the one that exceeds plenty.* There will always be some type of spark with someone out there that may hold such power over you seen as a light glowing especially for you. It is up to you to follow the light and see where it leads. There is no harm in searching for such a strong possibility.

Not to shut the world down with the simple fact of a "perfect world" not existing, but in our reality let's think realistic here. All it takes is that one person to ruin everything. There can be a huge concert going on with thousands of people and one person stands up, pulls out a 9mm and starts willingly shooting the crowd. The concert is over, ruined all because of one person. It's stuff like that which prevent the possibility of a perfect world being true. Let's simply have faith and make this world meaningful for what it's worth. Make it as perfectly set in stone as can be at least in our very own eyes until the entire world works as a team to make the whole planet a world of perfection.

"Perfect" is such a strong word. It is definitely used way too much nowadays. Even the One isn't perfect because we need flaws for conversation not confrontation. We need to learn from them and work as a team which actually builds up the relationship even further. Being "Perfect" is boring, we need something to work with. As we all strive for perfection in life, we are literally striving. Once we reach perfection, we want more. We Love it but want to reach perfection in something else. There is so much in life to accomplish that there are endless opportunities out there to reach.

Now the One exists for the simple fact of a stronger compatibility, stronger emotional connection and stronger togetherness. The One is as close as perfect as you will get. *Work together as One to reach perfection second to none. It is easier said than done.* Perform action and become close to "perfect".

Finding the One that came down from the sun will specially glow, mentally grow, be there to show perfection through the eyes of the connected soul. Light shines in the dark of the empty holes bringing life to a rise as lit up eyes and happy smiles expand the demise of that poor soul once alone in the hole. Now heavily rose from the ashes bold, bravery embraced, rich as gold all from the One Love offered emotionally told.

Chapter 17

Temptation

We all have our own temptations. *There may be girls or there may be guys that might tempt us to want to do sexual things. But we as people, especially the ones in a relationship must never give in.* Trust me it may be really hard (in a guy's case, literally) to not give in, but we need to control ourselves and our own urges. Too many people in this world can't and end up cheating. That is bad and not a good look at all. *Ball till you fall but you can never have it all!*

As Kevin Lyttle said "Tempted to Touch" is how some people feel when they want something so much and if you want a family and kids, only One can provide you with such. If a person is not satisfied with the One they are with, definitely do not waste time cheating because that will get you nowhere but a guilt trip down the drain, especially if a future is planned out with the presumed Love of your life. Temptation is not worth sacrificing Love.

There are times when someone feels tempted to attempt to do things disrespectful and relented at the same time as thinking right from wrong as a deceptive. Powerful minds of many kinds may feel more comprehensive, an incentive to open closed doors blocking the defensive. Boundaries collide and give you more of a perspective to test your ambition within your mission. It is your intuition to get rid of the suspicion. Remain and stay in your marital status position.

From a man's point of view, it is very hard to trust females to hang out with one on one while committed in a relationship because seduction is an obstacle to overcome. This may not apply to all females but yet it is unknown who stands where. It's way too easy for a female to make a move on a cute guy (relationship or not) so therefore it is best not to be in that situation period. Attraction always leads to temptation. There are more important things on a daily basis to achieve then fall into traps that you must escape from. *It's not worth getting trapped in a seductive attack. Stay on track with a Love that impacts.*

Knockout, boxing, poisonous toxins created in the mind to believe cheating is the option, defeating the purpose of Love existing if there is no emotional giving. Turn the clocks backward and begin a mental fixing to understand morals as a cleanse to create the right decision. Head on collision, direct heart incision shocking the brain to believe what you have and what is missing.

Define cheating? Cheating doesn't always have to be sexual intercourse. Cheating can also be secretly getting to know someone else on a personal level outside your relationship that your partner doesn't know about even if there is no kissing involved. There is no point in being in a relationship if you want more than the one that you supposedly Love. If you want to be a bachelor then so be it, but Love will never create itself as a result of that. Is Love something that you are ok with sacrificing?

For some it is very hard to stay faithful for the existence of sexual urges. They say curiosity kills a cat. Well, if you act on it then it definitely will kill a relationship.

Cheating isn't worth the time, energy or the way it appears to be because karma strikes hard affecting your mentality. It's not that hard. It's simply the reality for the heart to understand right from wrong, the whole morality. The ability to reach tranquility reflects on doing something right willingly to show your credibility because it is your responsibility.

There will be times when a person may feel that they can have it all. From one girl to the next or one guy to the next. It just really isn't worth it because in the end we all do not want to feel alone. As many people that a person gets with is a cycle that has its ups and downs. *It may feel good to concede because your experiencing a lot out there and fulfilling sexual needs. In the end, you can't have it all because it's simply all greed.* No one wants to be alone but being around a lot and cheating just isn't the way because there will always be moments when a person feels alone. If you are in a relationship and feel alone then obviously you are in a relationship with the wrong person. *Being happily in Love is the key to rid your life of sorrow and fill that void of loneliness for a better tomorrow.*

Alone on the phone with nobody home. So silent, so subtle, the possibility of cheating has grown. You may believe in something unknown that can be misleading to the morals you own but how you really feel may have a reason to make up or break up with the one that seems uneven but is really misunderstood for a person that is grieving. Your heart woke up and the tension is suddenly leaving. You hang up the phone and realize the one who really keeps you breathing.

Temptation is a devious way to pull in someone good and throw them out bad. Sounds like acts of the devil if you ask me. Let's not allow our ego to sky rocket above our urges because then the wrong decisions will be made.

Don't allow anybody to step in your way. *You control the path you choose. You control if you win or lose.* The decisions you make are powerful enough to make you or break you. Decide wisely, think logically and understand the circumstances that may result as an effect to the cause. Become better than the rest and become an inspiration to all just by making the right decisions in life. Become a leader for other people to follow so that they can become future leaders themselves. Lead the good to get rid of the evil demons that lurk in this world. *We can make this world better if we all become a team and work together!*

In a situation and high on expectation. Feels like segregation but faithful in duration. No time wasting, this is the presentation. Regain power and control to prevent what's wrong in those relations from all the right sensations. Sexual persuasion by disrespectful greed as shown throughout the nation when a single individual wants to get some for their own personal gaining. Become a leader, no cheating, surpass the obstacles of Temptation and a real inspiration for those who keep on hating.

Chapter 18

Aggression

Hulking rage embodies the soul to act aggressive, powering us up, enabling us to fight the good fight. Let's just stay away from the bad unnecessary ones that can ruin our lives because we definitely can't afford that. Allow Aggression to present itself in a morally correct manner instead of the cruel pointless acts of evil.

Aggressive acts of anger lead to an unstable decision making. The man/woman of someone's dreams may break their heart leaving them an emotional wreck left with an empty void fuming with aggression. We cannot let anything (especially when we are left heartbroken) impact our mind to perform poorly. It is usually a result of a Love being considered. What we think may be Love might or might not be Love. Breaking up after 10 years may seem harsh and question the true existence of Love itself.

We all become aggressive when something triggers our mind to blow a fuse causing an eruption of unknown proportions and distortions that leave us in misfortune. The anger of a person brings out the bad very often.

Do not let those negative demons interrupt who you are because if you lose yourself then you have just lost all that there is in humanity that this future needs to survive. If everyone lost their mind and became overly aggressive without a thought-out plan for technology to advance this civilization any further, we are screwed!

There is a heart broken, negative soaking, unfortunate sulking leaving you mentally open to anything out there that is controlling. Losing your mind for all that you were hoping. Someone out there still needs you to be coping with solutions to problems and not so provoking, but more so indulging to be more withholding by listening to the power we all are holding.

We have the power to let things in and let things go. Love will reveal itself and someday show. Let's not get it twisted with the wrong emotion because obsession and aggression impact the heart to act as a recession filled with the wrong intentions. No one wants to be in a relationship with someone who is abusive verbally or physically. Do not allow those wrong emotions to take control and falsely impact your willpower to turn against you. *Wherever there is a will there is a way. Love is here to stay but not accepted in the aggressive way.*

Control your anger and take deep breaths releasing all the tension within our chest rather than the open causing a mess. Deal with anger the right way to prevent all stress. Analyze thoughts more than for less creating the outcome to come out the best.

Be the best that you can be. Be the one to overcome the obstacles in the way. Use Aggression as a tool to enhance your adrenaline to rush and crush the walls blocking you from your destined future.

"You won't like me when I'm angry" said by the Hulk describes how most of us are when we actually become angry. The aggression from feeling like the strongest there is empowers you to become more savage. All you need is self-control to coexist with such aggression to become unstoppable. The beast within is there and must be tamed. Become WWE Superstar Brock Lesnar and conquer more than you did before.

We can be aggressive in a good way. We can be aggressive in selling, aggressive in playing sports, aggressive in bed and aggressive in taking control of tough situations. If something makes you feel depressed, brush those eyes off and become stronger. Use that hurt to build strength to overcome everything standing in your way. Remember, your toughest obstacle is You. Learn more about yourself. Figure out your strengths and weaknesses so that you can feel the power that you really do have.

Angry, mad, frustrated, sad, so much emotions that can drive you to act bad. Never allow yourself to fall out of character, have faith that an uplifting moment is there and will guide you in the right direction towards a happy future. Don't let your emotions get the best of you because there is always a light that shines in the dark. Never lose hope.

In a group of many, the aggressor will take a stand, outshine everyone as leader. No more cowardly acts, it is time to overcome being shy and make a name for yourself. *No one should ever doubt you because you are capable of so much more. Show the world what they have been waiting for.*

Relationships are very sensitive. Treat them with Love and care so that they do not break. Proceed with caution because one slip up can be the end of it all. Anger plays a huge role in relationships just as well as dates. No one likes to see people when they're angry, especially those who are in Love or are falling for that person. *Mental abuse can be just as bad as physical abuse depending on how far it goes. Be careful what you show to keep the connection strong with the ones you know.*

It is very important to be spiritually embraced by the person that you Like or Love because the embodiment of souls starts up the engine for a quick joy ride. *Cruising down the emotional lane will require consistent gas to fuel the heart and brain.*

Never forget how much you really do care because deep down inside you have a heart to spare. Too much at stake for a regretful future impacting the present reflected by the past. Make it worth it and make it last. Since we are human, we all have the power to change lives for the good and for the worse. Let's use that power to conquer anger and make a hero. We can be saviors if we use the strength we all are given to enhance relationships and embrace the world. *The world is awake and Love is at stake.*

Deception, intention and so many questions. Venomous injection reacts with Aggression. Hardcore anger and bottled up tension. Instinctive acts of pain, seamless recollection of disrespect, problems and so many to mention. Fight without fear in a life/death situation. In the end you fought for Love to appear a hero in your own mental spacing. Reality seeks the truth for nothing more than salvation.

THE STAGES OF LOVE

Chapter 19

The Stages of Love

There are stages to the process of Love. These stages are stairways that lead to the heavenly feeling itself, "Love".

The 1st stage is "Attraction". It is obvious that the moment you lay eyes on someone, there is always personal judgment about that person whether they are ugly in the face, you like their eyes, they have nice juicy lips, they have jacked up hair, there is a huge mole just chillin' on a cheek, are they a male or female?, your heart skipped a beat because of them, etc. All these are pure examples of opinionated thoughts that come to mind when you see someone especially for the 1st time. Usually ending up physically attracted to the other individual starts the Love process only because it is the beginning stage to it all. It is said that you can have only one 1st impression, well that impression is the one that lasts and makes or breaks a heart in an instant. In other cases when you get to know someone before even seeing them or speak to them more technologically rather than face to face then a different type of attraction may occur which is completely natural. Personality may overshadow appearance which proves that Attraction may exist in different forms. After being attracted to someone it may develop into liking them which is our next phase.

The 2nd stage is "The Liking Phase" aka "Puppy Love Phase" aka "Lust". When you generally like someone you are already attracted to them but think more of them. When you Like someone, you feel that they are a cool person that have a basic personality connected to their striking appearance which usually catches attention in the 1st place unless the person speaks in a way that overshadows a not so good appearance. Liking that person contributes a will to learn more and want more whether to be a sexy sight to see and/or shining personality that shows care. At a young age people tend to get this twisted with Love which makes it Puppy Love due to false allegations. Only due to the lack of experience these allegations are an occurrence of inexperienced knowledge. As time passes along with greater knowledge and experience, "The Liking Phase" is well known to be exactly what it is and not Love. This stage however can turn into "Lust" if there is such a huge physical attraction there. This can be bad if one person develops Lust and not the other. Lust is an overwhelming desire that can actually force someone to skip the 3rd stage and move on to stage 4 horribly wrong. If you are way too drawn physically and solely want pleasure, that can keep you from truly loving them. This may lead directly to "Obsession".

The 3rd stage is "The Emotional Phase". This is when a person surpasses "The Liking Phase" and develops feelings for the other person. This can be both good and bad because this stage involves internal pain. If one person reaches this stage before the other it may be difficult to coexist with until there is a balance between the two individuals. Something about that person's personality caught your attention enough to trigger the heart to create a spiritual vibe. Developing emotions are added to your daily routine. Focusing on work is one thing, focusing on a hobby is another thing, but focusing on a person emotionally is an addition that can spread out onto both. There has to be a balance due to what needs to get done and if your mindset is elsewhere then you are distracted. Allow emotions to fuel what needs to get done and not be a barrier blocking your way to success.

The 4th stage is "Obsession" which really is the trickiest stages of them all because if Obsession was created by Lust then it can never exceed this stage unless "The Emotional Phase" becomes born. To give birth to stage 3 in this predicament is extremely hard to create. The only way to do so is if you manage to get the other person to develop Lust. Obsession and Lust can create a balanced stage 3 which will cure a big headache. Now Obsession can go very wrong making this a tough stage because many people mistake Obsession for Love and that can be the downfall to a person if not resolved. Especially if Lust transformed into Obsession mistaken for Love, wow! That is way too much and can literally cause a person to act psycho. Please never mistake Obsession for Love because those are two different things. Feelings develop into Obsession which generally should be the good kind as for missing that person and thinking about that person deeply which will take you to the next stage.

The 5th stage is "The Deep Phase". This stage brings you to the point of strong emotion towards that person. Becoming an emotional wreck stuck in stage 4 for too long is really stressful. *Reaching this phase is more of a reward with guidance from the lord.* Always allow your Love for God to be #1 so that acceptance in finding a True Love will come true. Allow God into your life so that the right path is there for you to follow. *As deep as you can be, never forget that there is a light for you to see.* Your emotions really do matter and when deep feelings emerge, a notification that you really do care about this person does exist at this point. This honestly is a comfortable stage that actually may take a good amount of time to develop and lead to stage 6.

The 6th stage is "Love". It has been a journey to make it this far but reaching this stage is more of a fulfillment prospered by the word of God. *Finally reaching the goal seems to feel great but with emotion involved, turning back is too late. This is fate as thought about in this state. Time to create reason for the long wait. Love has arrived as desire through your eyes that only haters despise and only Lovers realize a well-deserved prize. Good people shall receive good things, it is defying karma as a minimal as intended for the visible. No need to be miserable when being alone should now be invisible.* Finally, fulfillment in your heart is now here. A balanced emotional life is intended to lead towards becoming husband and wife which leads into the final stage.

The 7th stage is "True Love". True Love is when both individuals are in Love and are deeply inseparable no matter what. It is rare that a lot of people reach this stage. This stage brings couples together forever. This stage can even be realized at an older age in life. Realizing this stage takes time to develop honest feelings that last. You may be in stage 6 with the thought of reaching stage 7 only for it all to break apart which meant that the 7th stage never had been reached to begin with. People tend to believe in this stage heavily while in the previous one only to not know exactly how sure until time shows the answer. Reaching this stage is Destiny. It can't become deeper than this. Knowing that you and your partner are in a balanced state of mind and at heart makes a person have no fear and the confidence to achieve almost anything. If a person doesn't already have that confidence in success, now they do! Sacrifices will be made and you have to give it 100% to remain in True Love so that you stay blessed in this stage forever and not temporarily.

So many stages, so many phases, your heart's beating fast as emotion escapes the cages trapped in your mind as feelings start engaging. The chapters of your life start developing pages that impact your soul that has been around for ages. Hearts begin to start raging and inspiring the next person that seems to be amazing. Connections made; the fear begins to fade as a Love is made in a story to be told through The Stages of Love as the emotions unfold.

POSITIVE POWER

Positive Power

Living in these hard times requires power, Positive Power. Power can be used for the good, but also for the evil. Sometimes money gives us power that is nothing more than greed. That's why there are the rich and powerful. It is great to be powerful but in a positive way. All the greed and negative energy will surely create a hole that you will eventually fall into and struggle to get out from. Why unknowingly make that hole to begin with? You can simply use the power that you have, whatever the case may be, in a positive force that can be used for the good and not the evil.

Feel the power from within a fun-loving person, not a tortured soul. *Too many crimes occurring on a global scale that must be prevented as a positive switch invented making the world a better place as God originally intended.* The power we all grasp can be really strong but even if so, must be in a positive way. *As an example, there may be a female so sexy, so fine, that she can get with any dude that waits in line.* Little do they know, she has extreme power but uses it negatively to control her personal needs sexually and materialistically. The power available can always go two ways, the right way of course is the positive way. The wrong way, you don't even want to know. All I can say is that it will eat you alive.

In the crime drama film "Juice" starring Omar Epps and Tupac Shakur, it shows how far someone will go to get power and respect. Bishop (Tupac Shakur) decides to do bigger things in order to win respect making him the most powerful individual of the group. While influencing his friends to go through with a robbery, it started causing problems in the group when Q (Omar Epps) had second thoughts. In the end it was almost like a battle of good and evil which resulted in Q having the most power. This shows two individuals using power in a good and bad way.

The wrong power from one person can break the heart of a powerful positive person causing them to be corrupted mentally and internally which can result in a power shift slowly erasing the positive energy they have been holding.

Suicidal in denial; striking the heart to shift in file. Look at the patterns on the tiles and connect the dots scattered for miles that make you realize where you have been for a while. Accept yourself as a person worthwhile who can't rewind time but move forward in style. Think positive, stay guarded, but understand Love as it all started.

Being obsessed or Loved by someone means that you have power over them. As it may feel good, it is actually healthy and better for there to be a balance in power if two people equally Love each other. Having extreme power over someone that is attached can trigger a side of you that normally won't show. If you are a leader you have to ask yourself, would you make greedy decisions? Would you make logical decisions? Is your decision a good one? Positively equal in power with the one you Love balances out those hard decisions you have to make just like a president with the assistance of a vice president or a general manager with the assistance of an operations manager.

Controlling the way you perceive your very own future is very significant for the next person that just may become inspired and follow through your very own footsteps. *A positive leader is what everyone in this world needs, not a dictator to proceed with greed and plant evil seeds that shower the world with the wrong needs.*

Not to bring some people down, but to be completely honest we are all living in a world where people unfortunately kill other people and commit suicide. It just seems nuts that people in this world actually do that and even if we have those thoughts it is all because we were lacking Positive Power at that very moment. We need positive energy from others to influence us and uplift us to pull through those tough times and become a better version of ourselves to overcome the difficult obstacles in our way. It should be in our best interest to remain positive at all times because that one time where you really can use that Positive Power but unfortunately have negative thoughts consuming you will be the downfall that can impact your entire life. Utilize your subconscious, morality, judgment, instinct and emotions to all help you regain the momentum towards that positive strength. *You have so much opportunity, so little time to waste. Do what's right in a thoughtful pace for a future to live in a life to be safe.*

Times have changed, solving problems is the game. This isn't math, no numbers to blame. No shame but only make a difference for the same that don't understand Love as a logical frame for two souls to connect on an emotional plane.

Deep down inside we all do have the power, it's just a matter of when to use it. It is recommended to not use it at all unless it is cleansed of all the negative energy contained. To get into the topic of Love on this aspect requires nothing but Positive Power in order for it to work and remain maintained. Losing Love just because of a power gone wrong will simply be a shame. Focus on the goal, think about the prize and notice the reward. True Love is the powerful destiny that most of us all strive for.

Always remember to never allow others to put you down. Never allow others to ruin your day and most importantly never allow anyone to make you act out of character. That will only drive you down the wrong highway leading to nothing but a dead end that you will have to fight to break out of. Analyze what's going on as it happens so that you can focus on something positive rather than exploding with negativity. Channel your energy so that you can use it in a good way to overpower the negative actions performed by others. *No one can stop you from getting in your way because you have the power to make this happen and have a good day!*

Positive Power, feeling empowered, so much hunger and the need to devour. Let the rain pour away in a negative shower so that the sun can become brighter for sight to actually matter. Feel your heart beating a mile an hour. Allow your body to feel strong so that you can climb the tower that is the life that we live to reach success in a timely manner.

CROSSING THE LINE

Crossing the Line

In life when it comes down to spitting game at someone you find attractive, making moves on a date or interacting with someone else other than your partner, there are limits otherwise you are Crossing the Line.

If you find someone attractive and end up approaching them, communicating and then feel the sudden urge or confidence to take it a step further, be careful so that boundaries aren't crossed. If you are already in a relationship and take the initiative to communicate for the reason of getting to know the person based on attraction then that is already Crossing the Line. You are in a relationship for a reason. There should be no reason to get to know another person in that sense. *It only leads into cheating and breakups. Too hard to makeup if you have already F'd up. Keep it real and keep it clean, honesty is the way to find the man/woman of your dreams.*

Approaching that attractive person that you had your eye on while not being tied down shows bravery and confidence. Scooping up the digits or leading into a kiss (if you and that person are actually that open) by all means proves that you got game! The life of a single person or a person in a relationship is very different. *Different perspective, different intentions as long as honesty is there*

101

to be shown and mentioned. If you are in Love or falling in Love then you should be well aware that there are boundaries involved point blank. Willing to exceed those boundaries proves that maybe Love just isn't for you. This is the harsh truth. We can't all be in Love, mess around with other people and get away with it. It just doesn't work that way.

The urge to mess around; a guilt that lurks around. A place you will be found once karma comes to town. Is this your last round? Boxing eventually ends, a fight that cannot be won if the rules were able to bend. Sucker punched to comprehend the boundaries that suspend the evil on the other end.

Dating is great from early to late. Never forget the start of the good times that await. Being on a date with that attractive male/female that you were dying to get to know is a great feeling but once your nerves kick in then that can break up the start of a new beginning. No one actually does know who the One for them actually is. When it comes to dating there are literally just two basic intentions:

1) Could he/she be the One for me?

2) Tonight am I going to smash?

When it comes to making moves on a date, you have to be careful. Already noticing a subliminal may already be enough for the "ok" to kiss. If the signs aren't clear, then depending on how tight your game is, you must be careful that you don't cross the line. This is how the dating world is designed; coming down to the moment of making a move and at the right time. We are trying to avoid a slap in the face or that awkward moment. *Remain confident, calm, smooth and ready to make a move only if the opportunity presents itself in a winning situation not to lose.*

We live the life of a risk taker. Every move counts and gambling is not what it's all about. *It's ok to gamble in life as long as it's not abused and that your thinking game is up to date with your confidence to amuse. Remain positive and never let yourself down and never let yourself go. Keep living your life and only time will show.*

In any occupation you work, you deal with the temptation of an attractive co-worker that you will have to deal with on a daily basis. Conversations on a professional level are bound to lead into personal conversations. You need to know the limits and especially your limits before you do something stupid. Getting to know someone can really mess with your emotions if you start to feel some type of way while in a relationship. That is when you need to fall back and keep yourself at a safe distance. Showing interest is the worst thing you can do if you are happily married with kids. Analyze the situation you are in and make well prepared decisions that you won't regret. Always think with your heart, never your head.

Never forget about the mistakes that you make because you will learn everything you need to learn from them to never make the big mistakes again. Learn more and grow strong.

Feeling intoxicated and high may alter your judgement and can lead to cheating. *If you are a strong individual that really cares about your partner in crime then you need to manage what you do on your spare time.* Defend your heart from the demons that attempt to possess us and make us angry and not think straight. Remember that a clear mind is the right mind.

Eyes lurking around without any sound, mentally focused but distracted by what's in your surrounding as your heart's pounding from attraction you've found. You find it profound to know you still got it but got someone tied down.

While in a relationship, if you are happy then you are good. If you are not happy then you must immediately consult with your partner about the issues you are dealing with. There must be an emotional resolution in order for the relationship to work. If you feel the need to cheat then just breakup. There is no point in keeping someone that you no longer want. If you are already happily engaged with a partner emotionally and physically and want more, you can't have more. There is only enough food for everyone. It is different if you are in a situation where you are in an open relationship or in a relationship with a bisexual, but unfortunately those don't last forever. True Love will never present itself with those complications involved. Two single individuals emotionally, spiritually and sexually involved with such strong feelings are in the pathway to True Love. The pathway is narrow enough for only two people, no matter what the weight because feelings and emotions weigh a ton.

Crossing the Line with someone that's fine is risking what's left behind. Dignity is blind when no thought left the mind in the decisions made, led with no sign. It's never too late to reconsider what's great because you never know if you are right on time. Time is there and there is hope. Hope that you can take an oath to make up what you were about to do wrong in a world where logic and morals may not be easy to cope. Do what's right, wash away the wrong but hold onto the soap.

Chapter 22

Drunk Love

After sipping on 200ml of Hennessy, I think this chapter shall begin. *Imagine being under the influence of alcohol while in a relationship and you're confronted by someone fine and divine that control seems to get out of line.* How strong is your Love towards your alleged other half when it comes down to a situation like this? Well your mind can only function to a certain extent while your heart can only function to an even lower extent and your private area will function to its fullest extent. How strong are you? How much can you control yourself? How deep are your feelings towards the One that is truly yours or how strong is your arousement? Which will prevail, Love or arousement? Only you can create that decision.

In the moment, sudden postponement when it comes to Love versus your sexual component. What is true? Is the sky blue or is it a fragment of your imagination because you had too much brew. Living in the moment may confuse the present in a fight for survival as the situation may seem pleasant. What flows in your heart that surges out your eyes as you suddenly despise what right from wrong implies under the influence as you fantasize.

Being in a situation where judgement is a virtue from within. You're fighting it as it sinks under your skin, allowing the truth to unfold and begin. The fight may be brutal as in the UFC but the result will come forth as justice or a sin to see. Be careful what you wish for because your heart, mind and soul may disconnect when drinking enters the realm to a tenfold. *Understanding the present, understanding the truth, what is right and what is wrong lies behind the booth.*

In the club, drinking, dancing, flirting and romancing. Limitations exist in the world of Love when feelings and emotions follow the steps of the bold. *Do not think with your private area as your mind starts to sink as the drinking will start to sync.* Become the man or woman that you are meant to be and be cautious of the decisions you make as you are having fun in the current state of mind. Do not leave your sanity behind because how you feel really impacts decision making to a breaking point. *Enjoy yourself, respect his or herself.*

One night stands may be tempting and grand, but waking up the next morning may be silenced and bland. Coming to a realization of the situation may impact your emotions as a complication. The truth always comes out when judgement kicks in. You will then know how you feel as a player or wife/husband.

Drinking, thinking, emotions are sinking but your conscience is there to cause all of the blinking to wake up from a dream with alot of rethinking. The moment held against the past may seem like a blast but time is running fast and the decisions will last. Become one of class and outlast the surpassed.

Any substance that can influence your judgement is powerful enough to become an interruption. Don't be a fool to something that can impact you in a negative way. Be the better man/woman that it takes to prevent all the mistakes that may lead to a break up or a bad decision that lowers your intuition.

Drinking Pink Moscotto helped me finish this chapter. It was the strongest drink to sip on in the refridgerator. Now to resume. *Living the way you want to live and living the way as intended need to be combined as a healthy balance for the future recommended.*

Understanding the position you're in whether it be in a relationship or single should be known to you and and the other person that you are talking to. The decision you make shouldn't come across as someone who just doesn't care but someone who actually thought through the decision made as a result of critical thinking.

How strong are you? Are you powerful enough to control the urges that make you don't give a f***? Living in the moment, drinking intoxicated stuff. Knowing how you feel and what you want seem tough, but the present assumes the future as it zooms faster in time as you sip and unwind. Relaxing in the moment as you start to find how you determine your next move as it was a crime but genuinely move towards what's going on in your mind.

Feeling like a mess as you drink away the stress may please you enough to sit back and confess. What really goes through your mind is hard as you remind yourself of what may seem redefined. Act simple and never make any situation complicated because it will only be a puzzle for you to solve in the end.

Be ready in the world we live in because our emotions and decisions impact our resolutions. We must fuse ideas and logic to overcome the obstacles that arise. *There are temptations that lay around and we must realize one from the next to move passed the duress.* As it all may seem like a simple thought process, it really isn't. Verbal fights may be a bad influence in your decision making and result in nothing but a fight between your conscience. This is a classic parody of a version of you that looks like a devil on one side and a version of you that looks like an angel on the other side. They clash by both influencing you in two different ways. It is your decision in the end for which path you follow but the good path is obviously the most ideal option. Think critically and choose wisely.

They say that the more you drink the more honest you become. Alcohol directly effects the brain, this changes the way you think, feel and behave. As the blood alcohol level in your system increases, your speech will become impaired and distorted balance. Your motor coordination, hearing and vision will become impaired.

You may feel depressed, not recognizing your impairments and experience increased confidence. That confidence makes it hard to be aware of ones limitations, this can lead to the poor choices.

As a part of Drunk Love, you must think from above as a logical choice towards the one you Love. That continues to arise as supremacy is victimized in the eyes of the one that will soon realize what is more civilized. In the moment to determine the more simplified decision for the future that is certain.

Chapter 23

Silence

When you are quiet, all you have are your thoughts. By shutting down your physical voice, it heightens your emotional voice. Speak loud and speak proud because the only person that can hear you is "You". To focus solely on your mental energy allows a stronger sense of emotional awareness to build up. *Create your very own world inside your mind and allow Love to awaken your soul to breathe from behind as a conscience hard to find.*

To actually get that alone time and shut down everything else may prepare you for your own self. We live in a multimedia world where accessibility makes it way too easy to be lazy. There was a time when we weren't as technologically advanced and smart devices didn't exist. Imagine living in the early 1900's when TVs just barely were invented and not even computers existed. Aside from work, all you have is the actual time to think to yourself about everything and everyone around you. *Look and listen through conversation and thinking. Love starts sinking as you are physically missing.* Silencing the world for a short period of time can't hurt if your emotions, thoughts and decision making powers up your body to act on time as it's waiting. *Don't wait, it is your fate to act now before it's too late.*

Say nothing, no hard thumping, no radio bumping and feel alive about something. Something special is about to be coming. A feeling like no other as you can feel your heart jumping. Suddenly what's quiet now starts crumbling, ground starts rumbling and hearing everything around you out in the open. Now that you got your mind right, you are now awoken.

Timing is everything and if you prepare for the next move it will be a good one. Don't always be instinctively quick with your actions because you cannot erase them. Actions are set and done. If you are on a date and reach in for that kiss, there is no turning back. Decide on the future that will arrive. Every second counts and leads to the reactions of what's about to be coming. *Whether they are good or bad, happy or sad, you have to toughen up and accept whatever's in the bag.*

WWE Superstar The Miz says "When my hand goes up, your mouth goes shut!" *That is clearly a disrespect to everyone but most still listen to what he has to say and respects his enthusiasm at the end of the day.* My point is that if you don't listen and don't pay attention, you will not understand anything. If you are on a date attempting to get to know that person but only talk about yourself, don't listen or learn anything about them, then you failed what you started and are incapable of Loving them. It is like talking to a statue with nothing in return. Listening to a person talk can actually create emotions that may eventually lead into Love.

Personality is the creation of unique characteristics about an individual and without it we would be living in a world with zombies and robots. It is the character of someone and how they think that makes everyone unique in their own way which attract certain people to them. Passion sticks to personality like glue. You can be on an interview, have little or no experience and get hired due to your personality and character. You can be on your very first date and get chosen to pursue something bigger due to your character and personality. An employer may Love the applicant's personality for the job. A date may Love the dates personality for a relationship.

Two different kinds of Love passionately linked to a personality. *With actual Silence, you can accomplish a lot and really understand what type of personality someone got.*

What lies behind a person's eyes is bigger than it is disguised. A mask not to be mistaken in size due to what's described. Heightened senses without fear to realize the truth to what lies. Experience what isn't seen to the naked eyes.

Think to yourself and really evaluate your thoughts. *If someone romantically pops up in your mind often, it will travel to your heart. This leads into an inner outburst of emotions that make the thought hard to part.* The same concept can be about a destination, an event, an item, a motive, etc. The big picture is that thinking about anything can lead to an emotion. You may be excited and anxious about any one of those concepts. Feeling Love for a person and feeling Love for something else can develop into two different things. When you really think about it, a lobster can't Love you back. It tastes good but it is in your stomach now. Such a random example, I know! Understanding the concept is all that matters. That person in front of you can respond with an emotion that can be shared together. This is what separates falling in Love with someone you are romantically or sexually attracted to or to something you strongly consider important.

As stated in Chapter 19 about the Stages of Love, one may develop an obsession mistaken as a lovely intention. Be on the lookout for stalkers, but be excited for Lovers. First glance can't distinguish the difference between a shy Lover and an obsessive stalker. When someone is silent, they are thinking to themselves and since we can't read minds, we must evaluate eye contact and movements to determine the comfort of becoming social on a personal level. Keep your guard up most of the time. *Lower down your defense when something truly does make sense.* Always have eyes in the back of your head. *Don't be dumb or naive. Think and breath before you believe.* Shyness and obsession are different. *Give the shy ones a chance before you judge at first glance.* Determine your path towards the future by being passionate, keeping your guard up and being real to yourself and others. *Live and learn before you allow the fire to burn!*

There is a Silence of the Lambs; horrific minds deserted in the sands. Confused about decisions but there is a Love that still stands. Obsessive thoughts from within struggling to reach the world as a sin. No more confusion; this is not an illusion. This is what you've been choosing as your heart starts improving. Wake up and start pursuing at the right timing that can lead to a shining but the light is far from blinding. The world must stop and allow peace to form a binding of the heart, mind and spiritual lining.

CHANGES

Changes

Imagine waking up every day and it feels like déjà vu;, living the same day over again where the sky is blue. Unfortunately, that is some of us. Alarm goes off, wash up, get dressed, drink coffee and go to work! I'm sure that is very similar to most of us but not all. *The logic of the same day repeating itself may not be appealing but something different will be revealing through how one is feeling.* One idea may inspire another which will impact someone else to repeat the same process of new ideas which will enhance society towards new beginnings. Through jobs, hobbies or just conversation, the impact you can leave on another person may affect a change. The change will affect the future. *It is our job to inspire others in a positive way so that the results lead into a good future for us to share someday.*

Allow your creative juices to flow and change what happens after the next blow so life doesn't beat you down as you fight for the next round. Every day is a battle between good and evil. You will either have a good day, a bad day or just another day. *All we can do is motivate and inspire the biggest desire in somebody's life to grow even higher.* The impact we make on someone will affect one life at a time if that person is empowered to inspire the next. For those of you who believe in karma, good things happen to good people. We hope to get that same support in return. The more Love we give, the more Love we will receive. *Make today count because tomorrow is not certain. Live life to the fullest to lift all the burdens.* Inspirational quotes were only created by us. *Let's inspire others to wake up, live and show the Love we want to give!*

Everyday creates the next; some better than the rest. Some stress; some less. Some sleep; some rest. Make moves to be the best so others can invest towards new ideas proclaimed. Learn and develop the skills gained. Push your hardest to progress and maintain. The future lies ahead and your heart holds the power of change!

Change is good; change is new. Change is a decision that we all must pursue. Changes happen and we know they're coming. How well we adapt to them is the true power. Getting transferred at your job, moving to a new home, having a baby or just falling in Love are many changes we all deal with. Love is definitely the most emotional one of them all. Are we willing to embrace it and act on it or just let it pass us by?

If you wake up on the wrong side of the bed, it does not mean you're going to have a bad day, it just means that something is different. There was a television series back in 2006 called "Day Break" starring Taye Diggs who portrayed Los Angeles Detective Brett Hopper who is stuck in a time loop; repeating the same day over and over. The series revolves around his attempt to solve the mystery of the murder of Assistant District Attorney Alberto Garza. The days get complicated with each decision he makes as he tries different tactics to find out who is behind the conspiracy to frame him. This series is the perfect example of decisions and consequences. Even though every day is the same, there is a change that always makes it different.

Probably the hardest thing to accept is when your companion or main squeeze has a change in emotion. *It is scary to know (emotionally and lustful), that one day you may receive so much affection and attention, the next day not as much. It's hard to misjudge and trust. A bad day can be distracting them from what appears to be fading away.* It is a hard pill to swallow if you are infatuated or deeply in Love with that person. *Whether it was short or long, the relationship wasn't as strong.* Being exclusive with someone for a few weeks or being married for a few years. *If you want something that bad, whether it be sex or Love, then you need to show how you feel through action to get a reaction worthy of.*

Do your part; do your job. Show someone how good you are at making them throb. Make life exciting; show them some lightning. Be welcoming and inviting, knowledgeable and delighting. Hanging out, phone calls, texting and writing will only last for how hard you are fighting!

If you are in a relationship or just getting to know someone, sometimes the texts, phone calls and visits just stop. *It doesn't always mean they're not interested. Sometimes being too busy is limited. The strength of the connection is what will determine if the emotions will fade or strongly escalate.* Don't forget that we hold the power of Change! We hold the power of Mjolnir! We are worthy like Thor! *We just can't control lightning or do anything supernaturally exciting.* The effort that you put in to maintain someone's attention requires work and is a job of its own to maintain what you want. We can influence the way a person thinks just based off conversation alone. *If you are smooth and make it easy to just open up, then there is a whole world full of exciting stuff. Just don't get carried away and make the wrong decisions that will create a bad day. Live life, make friends and have fun. Someday you will find that special someone that shines as bright as the sun.*

Life, what do we expect from it? A living, breathing body that we use to create experiences. The experience of Love and the experience of Change. *As time goes by, changes do occur as we go through the motions of a fading blur. Life goes on and we must live, laugh and have fun with all the Love that we can give.* As we grow into new experiences, that causes changes to occur. *The future is presented as we journey through time to live the life we intended.*

There are wages, rages, stages and phases. Never hold a burden to regret what a change is. Fight through it all to accept all the Changes. A battle through the ages; affecting your time against your design for how you define what you think is fine. Never forget but never regret the decisions you make for what's here at stake. Accept all mistakes but do not break. In the end, there is no escape.

THE
CONCLUSION
OF LOVE

The Conclusion of Love

In the end, nobody wants to be alone. In the zone, browsing on your phone and thinking all is good on your own. Being able to share your life experiences with someone is what most of us want. It is great to have time to yourself but also great to hangout and be social. In the movie "I Am Legend" a deadly virus originally created to cure cancer wiped out most of mankind, leaving Dr. Robert Neville as the last human in New York, other than the Darkseekers. Neville is immune to the virus and works to develop a cure while defending himself against those hostile mutants. *Being alone for years can have a huge mental impact on how you react.* That's why Neville began to talk to mannequins. We don't even need to go to that extreme because our soul mate is out there somewhere. Find yours and eliminate loneliness. *Nothing lasts forever except a Love shared together.*

We were created with purpose, with meaning and a reason for believing. Life cannot go on unless we create new life and grow civilization. We are not animals. We are human and that is what makes us powerful because we use our heart more than anything else. Making babies out of Love is ideal, but accidents do happen. It doesn't mean we will Love and cherish our babies any less but to create life out of purpose is truly something special. As far as technology is concerned, we advanced so much but cannot allow smart devices to be our downfall and make us look dumb. We are too intelligent to allow the laziness of technology take over our lives. Technology should be to enhance society, not make us mentally weaker. We allow each day to go by fast and forget to attend to the things we Love the most as much as we should. *Too much time away from what we Love will erase what we had emotionally created to think of.*

Never forget who you are. If you tell someone you need to find yourself and that you do not know who you are then you better get started on searching. Find out your purpose and why you were created to be on this Earth. What do you bring to the table? What are your skills and what are you good at? What are you willing to do? How far will you go to get what you want? How far will you go to help others? Many questions can challenge you to think about the who, what, when, where and why. No question does not have an answer. What's yours?

It is shocking to know that there is a delusional disorder called Erotomania. Problematic behaviors include actions such as calling, sending letters, gifts, making unannounced visits and other persistent behaviors. That sounds like a lot of people in this world. Are we living in a world of denial or are we suffering to accept the fact that obsession overrules Love? Not everyone is meant for you. Sometimes we cannot always get what we want. It could be a sign that it is not meant to be or it could be an indication that you need to fight harder for what you believe in. *To determine that is up to you but there is no turning back for what you're about to go through.* Learn when to give up because not every battle will result in a win, that is just how life works. If you are not strong enough than you are just not strong enough. We are not "The Incredible Hulk" and cannot smash through every obstacle. If he or she does not Love you as you Love them then you really need to think hard if it's worth the fight anymore. For the most part, we do not live in a world with fairy tale endings. We live in a world where fairy tale endings are portrayed as fantasy. *All we can do is live our lives and survive the hard times to move forward and not rewind.*

How do you really conclude what Love is? *Understand what type of emotions you feel and determine fake from real.* You and the other person must be on the same page to build the bond that you share. *Love comes and goes. All you can do is go with the flow. If you can reach the pinnacle for what Love truly is then you must surrender your heart to maintain and give.* Both individuals must feel the same for this to work. *We don't want to live in a world to surrender souls but our heart is the key to fill all of the holes. Listen to your mind, follow your heart and breathe through your soul to create what you want to be told.* Everyone has a story. Sometimes it's good and sometimes it's bad. The Conclusion is what we wait for. Create the story you want to be shared.

Our life is like a movie that never ends. There are sequels or reboots, even in our minds. A decade may pass and a movie may be told differently or a sequel to what's next. In life, we conclude what's next even though we can't predict the future. We can do our best creating one. We work hard to provide, enjoy life and have a family worth living for. We strive for a long life and live it how we want to, single or married. The choice is ours but if we have that mentality that Love is out there, it will come. *You can ether wait for it, search for it, find it, keep it, throw it away or live a life wondering what is out there for you someday.* To be brutally honest, Love does not last forever and not everyone will be lucky enough to find it. A lot of people claim that they were in Love and fell out of it or stories about their first Love. All of that may be true but do not forget anything about Chapter 19 dealing with The Stages of Love. *Feel what is real.*

Sometimes we want someone erotic; someone exotic, but in the end, we really just want someone to rock with. To keep all of our thoughts to ourselves only creates a buildup which may lead to an outburst someday. At least talking to someone you trust can release those emotions little by little. The desires we hold are only temporary. Building a relationship and having children is how life moves on. Most of us want that and most of us want a marriage to last forever. That is difficult these days and brings me back to fairy tales being perceived as a fantasy. There still is hope because a lot of our grandparents shared a Love that did seem to last forever.

There are 3 types of people in this world:

1) Live life to the fullest, be single and have fun

2) Search for the One and hope to find them someday

3) Live a happy life with your companion and kids

There are also people that combine those elements. *You are living life to the fullest, having fun being single but still express interest to search for a Love interest. If you are living a happy life with your companion and kids but look to have fun and live life for more than it is, be careful not to slip up with your Mr./Mrs. If you still live that happy life but search for something more, then you are in denial for what you're asking for.* Balance out the 3. *Have fun but live life in hopes to find the One. Be happy as can be when Love sets you free.*

Don't ever feel "tied down" when you are in a relationship. *You should feel the opposite if the trust is there. Attention, affection and care with a sexual flare make you feel Love in the air.*

As we wake up every morning, most of us don't wonder what is missing. We live day by day lives and wake up to work, only to come home to work if we want a relationship to work. All that requires work.

We live a life where we go through different phases in all the stages to reach Love. *We are mentally trapped in a puzzle as we struggle to reach the end of the tunnel. We will see the light and make God proud if we live a life worth living to reach a Love that is fitting.*

Remember to always be happy, passionate and true as you decide the type of Love that well suits you. In a world full of fun and adventure, we create the future that we want together. We Love life, Love people and Love what makes all of us equal. Create the sequel to your Love story. Inspire others and make the future meaningful!